THE IMPORTANCE OF

Richard M. Nixon

by
Roger Barr

Lucent Books, P.O. Box 289011, San Diego, CA 92198-9011

These and other titles are included in The Importance Of biography series:

Benjamin Franklin
Chief Joseph
Christopher Columbus
Marie Curie
Galileo Galilei
Richard M. Nixon
Jackie Robinson
H.G. Wells

Library of Congress Cataloging-in-Publication Data

Barr, Roger, 1951–
    Richard M. Nixon / by Roger Barr.
    p. 112—(The Importance of)
    Includes bibliographical references (p.107) and index.
    Summary: A biography of former president Richard Nixon, beginning with his youth, continuing through his presidency, the Watergate Affair, and his life today.
    ISBN 1-56006-035-2
    1. Nixon, Richard M. (Richard Milhous), 1913–   —Juvenile literature. 2. Presidents—United States—Biography—Juvenile literature. [1. Nixon, Richard M. (Richard Milhous) 1913– 2. Presidents.]   I. Title.   II. Series.
E856.B36   1992
973.924'092—dc20   92-25566
[B]   CIP
                                                                              AC

Contents

Foreword

THE IMPORTANCE OF biography series deals with individuals who have made a unique contribution to history. The editors of the series have deliberately chosen to cast a wide net and include people from all fields of endeavor. Individuals from politics, music, art, literature, philosophy, science, sports, and religion are all represented. In addition, the editors did not restrict the series to individuals whose accomplishments have helped change the course of history. Of necessity, this criterion would have eliminated many whose contribution was great, though limited. Charles Darwin, for example, was responsible for radically altering the scientific view of the natural history of the world. His achievements continue to impact the study of science today. Others, such as Chief Joseph of the Nez Percé, played a pivotal role in the history of their own people. While Joseph's influence does not extend much beyond the Nez Percé, his nonviolent resistance to white expansion and his continuing role in protecting his tribe and his homeland remain an inspiration to all.

These biographies are more than factual chronicles. Each volume attempts to emphasize an individual's contributions both in his or her own time and for posterity. For example, the voyages of Christopher Columbus opened the way to European colonization of the New World. Unquestionably, his encounter with the New World brought monumental changes to both Europe and the Americas in his day. Today, however, the broader impact of Columbus's voyages is being critically scrutinized. *Christopher Columbus*, as well as every biography in The Importance Of series, includes and evaluates the most recent scholarship available on each subject.

Each author includes a wide variety of primary and secondary source quotations to document and substantiate his or her work. All quotes are footnoted to show readers exactly how and where biographers derive their information, as well as provide stepping stones to further research. These quotations enliven the text by giving readers eyewitness views of the life and times of each individual covered in The Importance Of series.

Finally, each volume is enhanced by photographs, bibliographies, chronologies, and comprehensive indexes. For both the casual reader and the student engaged in research, The Importance Of biographies will be a fascinating adventure into the lives of people who have helped shape humanity's past, present, and will continue to shape its future.

Important Dates in the Life of Richard M. Nixon

Nixon is born in Yorba Linda, California.	**1913**	Graduates from Whittier College in California; enters Duke University Law School; graduates third in his class in 1937.
Defeats incumbent Jerry Voorhis for the California Twelfth Congressional District seat.	**1934**	
	1946	Suspected communist spy Alger Hiss makes his first appearance before the HUAC. Nixon's pursuit of Hiss captures headlines.
Defeats Helen Gahagan Douglas in California for United States Senate seat.	**1948**	
	1950	
Nominated for Vice-President at the Republican national convention.	**1952**	Inaugurated as Vice-President of the United States.
President Eisenhower suffers heart attack; Nixon briefly assumes presidential duties.	**1953**	
	1955	In Peru and Venezuela, crowds attack Nixon; he receives a hero's welcome upon his return to Washington.
Nixon and John F. Kennedy participate in the first of four televised presidential debates; loses close presidential election to Kennedy.	**1958**	
	1960	Loses governor's race in California; *Six Crises* is published.
Elected to be the thirty-seventh president of the United States.	**1962**	
	1968	Announces U.S.– South Vietnamese invasion of Cambodia; four students die during Kent State University protest on May 4.
Visits China; attends summit conference in Moscow; signs the first arms reduction agreement between the United States and the Soviet Union; Watergate scandal begins; elected to a second term as president.	**1970**	
	1972	Announces peace agreement with North Vietnam; the Senate begins televised Watergate hearings; John Dean implicates Nixon in the Watergate cover-up; Alexander Butterfield reveals existence of Nixon tape-recording system.
	1973	
House of Representatives begins inquiry on impeachment of Nixon; U. S. Supreme Court orders Nixon to turn over tapes subpoenaed by the special prosecutor; on national television, Nixon announces he will resign the presidency.	**1974**	
	1976	Visits China and receives warm welcome, even though he is ignored in the United States.
	1978	
Publishes his memoirs and declares he is "out" of exile.	**1980**	*The Real War* is published.
	1986	
Cover story in *Newsweek* magazine proclaims Nixon's rehabilitation.	**1989**	Nixon criticizes presidential candidates for ignoring foreign policy and aid to the former Soviet Union; leading candidates respond with aid proposals.
Nixon departs for China to communicate U. S. disapproval of Tiananmen massacre.	**1992**	

A Bitter Legacy

Perhaps more than any other president in recent memory, Richard Nixon stands out in the public's consciousness. His accomplishments and foibles generated sweeping changes in politics, the media, and in the scope of presidential power. Nixon's attempt to cover up the Watergate break-in launched a new approach to political coverage—investigative reporting. Because of his stubborn reluctance to release subpoenaed tapes during the Watergate investigation and because of his handling of the Vietnam War, an angry Congress passed laws limiting presidential power. In spite of being a staunch anti-communist, Nixon improved diplomatic relations with communist regimes of the Soviet Union and China because world stability depended on it. And, although Nixon was forced to resign and left the presidency in shame, he has played an important advisory role to several presidents, George Bush and Ronald Reagan among them, and his ideas continue to influence current affairs.

Richard Nixon's legacy, therefore, while vast, is also overwhelmingly mixed. Nixon is best known not for the positive influence he had, but for his domestic failures and his actions as president during the bitterly divisive final months of the Vietnam War.

For most Americans, then, Nixon's legacy is one of failure. Yet he remains well-liked and respected outside this nation,

Nixon meets with Communist party leader Leonid Brezhnev. As U.S. president, Nixon opened relations with both the Soviet Union and China.

Despite his repeated scandals, Nixon continues to be respected by other politicians.

especially among the people of China and the former Soviet Union. He also continues to exercise respect among politicians today. This is also part of Nixon's legacy.

The final historical judgment on Nixon's presidency has yet to be determined by historians. Americans are still too close to the events that Nixon influenced to truly think objectively about his contributions. Yet, in some ways, Nixon's story is tied to the story of the maturing of the American people. In the years of Nixon's presidency, the American people grew up, lost some of the innocence and shine that, however naive, seemed to embody America. In part because of Nixon, Americans view politics with less idealism, and with more skepticism and depth.

In *The Importance of Richard M. Nixon*, Nixon's accomplishments and foibles are examined and evaluated. How Nixon will ultimately be remembered, and which of these legacies will endure, will be left to future generations.

Chapter

1 Young Richard Nixon

Richard Milhous Nixon was born on January 9, 1913, in Yorba Linda, California, in a small house built by his father. He was the second of five sons born to Francis A. (Frank) Nixon and Hannah Milhous Nixon. During Richard's earliest years, the Nixon family ran a small lemon ranch in Yorba Linda that Hannah's family had helped them establish. The lemon ranch failed to prosper, however, and both parents worked at other jobs to support the family. In 1922, the Nixon family moved to nearby East Whittier, where Frank Nixon opened a gasoline station. Soon, he added a grocery store. The hours were long and the work difficult. Each of the Nixon boys grew up working in the store.

Even as a young child, Richard Nixon was special, according to his mother.

> Richard's father and I could see, from the first, that Richard was a gifted child. We wanted him to be somebody . . . I thought he would be a musician, for he had a natural ear. . . . When Richard was ten, I sent him to live with my sister, Jane Beason, a piano teacher, so that he could study with her. The year before, however, Richard had already, in a childlike sort of way, announced that he was going to be a lawyer. One day in the house at Yorba Linda, when

Richard was nine, and the newspapers were full of stories about the infamous Teapot Dome lawyer-bribery scandals, Richard . . . told me, "Mother, when I get big, I'm going to be a lawyer they can't bribe."[1]

Richard Nixon spent his early childhood on his family's lemon ranch in Yorba Linda, California.

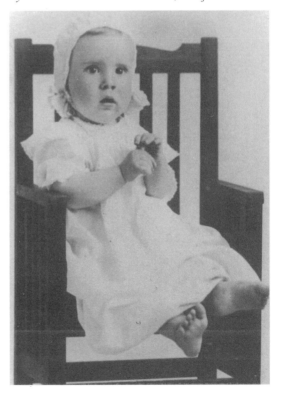

Parental Influence

Nixon's parents were very different from each other. His father was born into a poor Ohio family. He left school after the sixth grade and worked at various jobs in Ohio before moving to California. Outgoing, even gregarious, Frank worked hard to support his family. He was tight with money and refused any type of assistance he considered to be charity. Discussing the Bible and politics were among his passions. Frank Nixon was also a crude, angry man noted for his explosive temper.

Hannah Milhous, on the other hand, came from a well-respected Quaker family and had attended college. She was a quiet, religious woman with a peaceful nature that balanced her husband's volatile one. She, too, worked hard to raise her boys and to help make ends meet.

In his memoirs, Nixon recalled:

I loved my parents equally but in very different ways, just as they were very different people. My father was a scrappy, belligerent fighter with a quick, wide-ranging raw intellect. He left me a respect for learning and hard work, and the will to keep fighting on no matter

A Chronically Angry Man

The hidden influence of Hannah and Frank Nixon on their son was recorded by Fawn Brodie in Richard Nixon: The Shaping of His Character.

"But Frank Nixon was a chronically angry man, ulcer-ridden from the early years of marriage, crude, and brittle, who invited hatred in his own family. He had, indeed, a talent for survival, but it was for survival without love. This talent Richard would learn from him.

Mostly, however, the son consciously tried to be as unlike his father as possible. Where Frank shouted, Richard prided himself on being 'the coolest man in the room.' Frank was untidy . . . Richard from his earliest years was fastidiously clean. . . .

Nixon feared and disliked his father as loud, brutal, and sometimes dirty, but Frank was also preeminently masculine. For Richard to be cool, fastidious, and quiet was to be like his mother. He would put his mother's manners into the service of his father's objectives. The need both to feel proud of his father and to show that he was unlike him—to redeem him by being successful and by the same token to surpass him, showing his lack of worth—stayed with him well into the presidency."

The Nixon family, including (from left to right) Harold, Frank, Don, Hannah, and Richard. The family ran a grocery store and gas station (pictured above) after their lemon ranch failed.

what the odds. My mother loved me completely and selflessly, and her special legacy was a quiet, inner peace, and the determination never to despair.[2]

Frank and Hannah Nixon's dissimilar backgrounds and personalities made their marriage an explosive one that filled the household with tension.

There were frequent conflicts between family members. In the store, Richard and the other boys would try to outshout their father. Customers of the gas station and grocery store would be shocked as Frank and the boys quarreled bitterly in front of them.

Richard's mother handled family conflicts very differently from her husband. Although she seldom raised her voice, she imposed a quiet discipline that Richard and his brothers came to dread almost as much as Frank's belligerent methods. When her husband made an unpopular ruling on an issue, Hannah avoided confrontation. Instead, she quietly manipulated the situation until she achieved more satisfactory results. As he grew up, Richard also learned to avoid his angry father, staying out of sight until his temper cooled.

The Nixons' difficult marriage affected the family in other ways. Hannah would sometimes become so frustrated with her life that she would leave home, returning to the Milhous household for extended periods. Young Richard's feelings of abandonment as a result of these incidents surfaced in a letter he sent to her when he was eleven. In the letter, he cast himself as a mistreated dog. He concluded the letter, "I wish you would come home right now. Your good dog Richard."

There were other influential events in Nixon's early life. In July 1925, when Richard was twelve, his seven-year-old brother, Arthur, became sick and died a few days later. In his memoirs, Nixon wrote that

The Nixon brothers, (from left to right) Harold, Richard, Arthur, and Don. Arthur's death at the age of seven may have spurred Richard to succeed.

the loss of his brother was the first time he learned what death meant. His mother recalled that Arthur's death established a pattern in the way her son dealt with tragedy and marked a change in his character.

During Arthur's illness, I had sent Harold, Richard and Donald to stay at Mr. Nixon's sister's house in Fullerton. I can still see Richard when he came back. He slipped into a big chair and sat silent and dry-eyed in the undemonstrative way in which, because of his choked, deep feeling, he was always to face tragedy. I think it was Arthur's passing that first stirred within Richard a determination to help make up for our loss by making us very proud of him. . . . Now his need to succeed became even stronger. . . . In elementary school, in college and in law school, Richard was always one of the two or three students at the head of the class.[3]

Nixon's Character

Richard attended first Fullerton, then East Whittier High School. He was awkward and shy, a good student who worked very hard at his studies. He tried out for football but proved to be such a poor athlete that he seldom got to play. Rather than quit, Nixon displayed the never-say-die attitude he had learned from his father. By continuing to work at developing his skills and cheering on others from the sidelines, Richard earned the admiration of his teammates.

He joined the debate team and became one of the school's best debaters. His teacher noticed that his debate tactics were different from those of the other students. Richard "had this ability to kind of slide

Opposites Attract

Nixon described his parents and their influence on him in his memoirs, published in 1978.

"The principle that opposites attract aptly describes my mother and father. In the most important ways they were very much alike. Both were deeply religious. They were completely devoted to one another, and no sacrifice was too great for them to make for their children. But two more temperamentally different people could hardly be imagined. . . .

My father had an Irish quickness both to anger and to mirth. It was his temper that impressed me most as a small child. He had tempestuous arguments with my brothers Harold and Don, and their shouting could be heard all through the neighborhood. He was a strict and stern disciplinarian, and I tried to follow my mother's example of not crossing him when he was in a bad mood. Perhaps my own aversion to personal confrontations dates back to these early recollections.

My mother was always concerned and active in community affairs, but her most striking quality was a deep sense of privacy. Although she radiated warmth and love for her family, indeed, for all people, she was intensely private in her feelings and emotions. We never had a meal without saying grace, but except for special occasions when each of us boys would be called on to recite a verse from the Bible, these prayers were always silent. She even took literally the injunction from St. Matthew that praying should be done behind closed doors and went into a closet to say her prayers before going to bed at night."

Frank and Hannah Nixon at their wedding.

around an argument instead of meeting it head-on," she recalled, a tactic similar to the indirect, manipulative methods the family used to deal with Frank Nixon. Just as Frank Nixon had successfully argued with friends over political issues, young Richard "could take any side of a debate with such technical skill." The teacher's observation that there was something "mean in the way [Richard] put his questions, argued his points" was similar to observations made about Frank Nixon.

In his senior year, Richard ran for president of his class. He lost the election, a defeat that stayed with him for more than fifty years. In his memoirs, he would refer to that election as his first political defeat.

After graduating from high school, Nixon hoped to attend an eastern college. However, his older brother Harold was ill with tuberculosis, which strained the family's finances. Instead of going East, Richard enrolled at Whittier, a local Quaker college, and began his freshman year in 1930.

Richard excelled in college as he had in high school. He continued to participate on the debate team and developed a reputation as a fierce opponent. He tried out for college football, but his mediocre playing meant that he was allowed to play only when the outcome of the game had already been decided. Yet his stubborn determination not to quit impressed his coach and teammates. Richard also acted in college plays. His acting teacher encouraged him, seeing in Richard a natural ability.

He kept active in the social side of school as well, starting his own fraternity called the Orthogonians. As a senior, he ran for class president. The central issue of the campaign was whether dancing should be allowed on campus. Nixon did not dance himself but promised to bring dancing to

Richard Nixon's high school senior portrait. He graduated from East Whittier High School in 1930.

Whittier if elected. He won the election, and his defeated opponent would later refer to him as a "smart politician."

Nixon graduated second in his class from Whittier College. After interviewing many of Nixon's former classmates, biographer Roger Morris noted that students viewed Nixon in various, contrasting ways:

There sometimes seemed two Richard Nixons, the one prominent and familiar, the other almost opaque or unseen. Scores of students knew him as the now imposing, now awkward campus leader, scholar and actor, debater, and football bench warmer, the brisk, intent young man hurrying from activity to activity. Many saw him much closer, behind stage or on the football field or in

Not Much of a Mixer

In Good House-keeping *magazine in June 1960, Richard Nixon's mother, Hannah, described her son as a boy.*

"Richard, as a boy, was not much for social chatter—or any other kind of talk. He was so tight-lipped, as a matter of fact, that he could always be trusted with a secret. And he was also reticent when it came to such social affairs as picnics; he used to say that people took home, from among the leftovers, more food than they had brought with them in the first place. As far as I know, Richard was not much of a mixer in college, either. He never had any special buddy, and on what dates he had during his college years he talked not of romance but about such things as what might have happened to the world if Persia had conquered Greece or what might have happened if Plato had never lived."

Hannah Nixon with her three surviving sons.

Orthogonian meetings, as a solitary, shy, painfully uncertain boy amid all the apparent energy and versatility.[4]

During his college years, another death shook the Nixon family. Throughout his years in high school and college, Richard's brother Harold had suffered from tuberculosis. Early in Harold's life, his condition became so serious that Hannah had taken him to a colony in Prescott, Arizona, to get well, leaving Richard and the remaining boys behind. In July 1933, Harold died. Hannah again saw a change in Richard after Harold's death. The loss, she observed, had a lasting effect on him:

> He sank into a deep, impenetrable silence. From that time on, it seemed that Richard was trying to be three sons in one, striving even harder than before to make up to his father and me for our

Harold Nixon's tuberculosis became so severe that he was sent to a convalescent home in Arizona. He died of the disease in 1933.

loss. With the death of Harold his determination to make us proud of him seemed greatly intensified. Unconsciously, too, I think that Richard may have felt a kind of guilt that Harold and Arthur were dead and that he was alive.[5]

After graduation, Nixon received a scholarship to attend Duke University Law School, and in 1934, he went East to North Carolina to begin his studies. The classes at Duke were difficult, and Nixon nearly quit and returned to California. But he did not give up and completed his first year. As the year ended, Nixon was so concerned about his grades that he and another student broke into the dean's office to check their grades before they were released. Nixon never mentioned the incident in his memoirs, but biographer Roger Morris observed that the break-in

A Split Between Word and Deed

Historian Fawn Brodie discusses in Richard Nixon: The Shaping of His Character *how his personality developed.*

"To understand what caused the splitting between word and deed in Nixon's life we must go back to his childhood, adolescence, and early career. These years give us clues, too, to the evolution of other major aspects of Nixon's life, his loneliness, his sense of being an outsider, his distrustfulness, his lack of a real sense of identity, his delight in acting, his inclination always to be on the attack, and his narcissism. But along with the darker aspects of Nixon's psyche we will see the evolution of the image so many found attractive: the earnest young moralizer, the ardent patriot, the enunciator of virtue, the defender of clean living and sanitized language. The maintenance of this image was one of the necessities of Nixon's life."

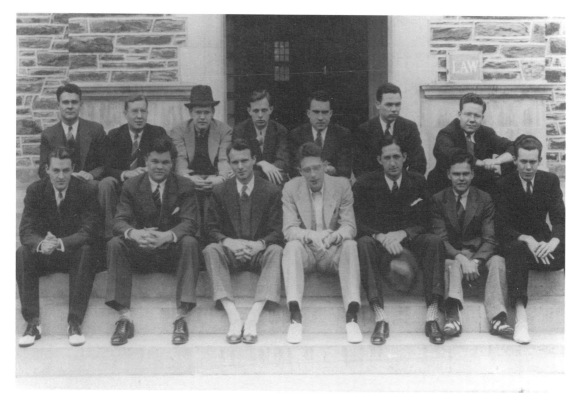

*Richard Nixon (fifth from left, top row) with the Duke law honor society
in 1937, the year he graduated with his law degree.*

was in its way a telling mark of the taut,
pressured young man Dick Nixon had
become and was becoming at twenty-
three. It silhouetted the fragile sense of
self that lay near the surface of his tena-
cious discipline, and unease that drove
him at . . . Duke and elsewhere to gen-
uine, reputable achievement and sometimes, in ways . . . small and large, to a
fugitive, self-defeating recklessness.[6]

In his three years at law school, Nixon
continued to follow the study habits he
had established in high school and college. Upon graduating from Duke, Nixon
first tried to secure a job in New York City,
failed, then returned to California. He
joined the Whittier law firm of Wingert

and Bewley in November 1937. His law
career got off to a tough start. One of his
first cases resulted in a malpractice suit
filed against the firm, due in part to mistakes Nixon had made.

A Career in Politics

After his rocky start, Nixon quickly settled
into his law practice. The firm handled
business matters, wills, and other routine
cases. Although Nixon proved to be a ca-
pable attorney, his heart was not in his
work. His real interest was politics. With
the same discipline he had harnessed during his academic career, Nixon plunged
into local politics.

Nixon served in the South Pacific during World War II as an officer in the U.S. Navy.

He joined numerous civic organizations. He led the Whittier and Duke alumni groups and served with the local Kiwanis. He was a member of the chamber organization of the nearby community of La Habra. Later, he campaigned behind the scenes to become the La Habra city attorney, but the community leaders refused to discharge the incumbent.

Disappointed, Nixon did not give up. Hearing that his district representative in the California Assembly might not seek re-election, Nixon quietly began campaigning to small groups and organizations. His fledgling campaign stalled when the incumbent decided to run for office again.

But Nixon was looking far beyond local politics. During the winter of 1939 and 1940, he told at least one colleague that he would someday be president of the United States. His political career was put on hold, however, when World War II intervened.

A month before the December 7, 1941, Japanese attack on Pearl Harbor, Nixon took a job in Washington, D.C., with the Office of Price Administration (OPA). He worked as a lawyer in the OPA's tire rationing division. The position, as he recorded in his memoirs, "seemed a good opportunity to go to Washington and observe the working of the government firsthand."

Eight months later, Nixon applied for an officer's commission with the U.S. Navy and entered the service in August 1942. Nixon served in the South Pacific, then returned to the United States to help wind down the government's war effort. Using his legal skills, he helped terminate contracts for war supplies that the government had signed with hundreds of American manufacturers.

In September 1945, shortly before his discharge from the navy, Nixon received a letter from a group of Whittier businesspeople that changed his life. They wanted him to replace their district's Democratic representative in Congress. During his years in Whittier before the war, Nixon had impressed the business community as a bright, conservative young man and a tireless campaigner.

Nixon wrote back that he was indeed interested. His reply marked the true beginning of his political career. During the next forty years, Richard Nixon would travel far beyond his California district and make history. He would become both famous and infamous. He would be loved and hated in the United States and around the world.

2 The Rise to Power

Richard Nixon's decision to run for Congress in 1946 marked the beginning of his dramatic rise in American politics. In just six years, he would be catapulted from the obscurity of local California politics to become the Republican party's candidate for vice-president of the United States. Along the way, Nixon would capture the nation's attention and help define public attitudes about communism.

Nixon's opponent in the Twelfth District race for Congress in 1946 was the incumbent, Jerry Voorhis. Voorhis, a Democrat, had first been elected to Congress in 1936. He was respected by his fellow congressmen and was generally considered unbeatable.

Nixon, however, believed he could beat Voorhis. In his memoirs, Nixon recalled:

> The greatest advantage I had in 1946 was that the national trend that year was Republican. People were tired of the privations and shortages of four years of war, and in the burst of postwar prosperity they were beginning to bridle against the government regulations.[7]

Nixon also attacked Voorhis's character. Nixon's political consultant, Murray Choitner, studied Voorhis's record in Congress and turned it against him, portraying Voorhis as an ineffective legislator.

Early in the campaign, Nixon's campaign organization began sending a steady flow of articles slanted in his favor to the local newspapers. Many of these articles were published as written, bias and all. Nixon also received the endorsement of the district's largest newspaper, the *Los Angeles*

Nixon defeated Jerry Voorhis, an incumbent congressman, in 1946 by using publicity and false accusations to discredit his opponent.

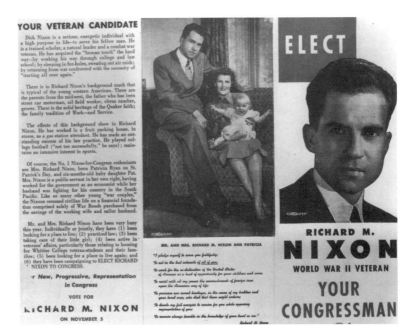

Advertisements and biased newspaper articles helped Richard Nixon win the congressional campaign of 1946.

Times. As a result, coverage of the Nixon campaign soon dominated the local press. Throughout the campaign, Nixon enjoyed extensive press coverage, while Voorhis struggled to get his views into print.

To get more publicity for his own views, Voorhis offered to debate Nixon early in the campaign. Nixon prepared carefully for each debate with Voorhis and, using his old debate skills, demolished his opponent.

But by far Nixon's most effective campaign tactic was to exploit Americans' emerging fear of communism, a political system that favors ownership of all property by the government. In 1946, communism was perceived as a threat to U.S. national security. Because the United States and the communist Soviet Union were enemies after World War II, Americans feared an attack by the Soviet Union. Also, because of fears of communist spy activities, members of the Communist party within the United States came under suspicion.

In his campaign, Nixon tried to portray Voorhis as a politician with communist ties. At the core of Nixon's attack was his deliberate blurring of the distinction between two separate political action committees (PACs). A PAC is a group that represents the political interests of an organization or business. One PAC had communist ties while the other did not. Nixon claimed that the PAC with communist ties had endorsed Voorhis, when, in fact, the other PAC had made the endorsement. In one of their debates, Voorhis denied that he had been endorsed by communists. Nixon then produced stationery from both PACs and pointed out that even though the two groups were different, they had some of the same individuals on their respective boards of directors. These shared individuals, Nixon charged, made the groups' political goals the same.

Nixon's charges that Voorhis was endorsed by communists were false. Voorhis's record in Congress showed that he was a strong anticommunist. Yet Nixon's skillful maneuvering convinced the public otherwise, and Voorhis was unable to overcome the stigma.

Nixon used other tactics to reinforce the false link between Voorhis and communism. Nixon volunteers telephoned many voters in the Twelfth District. The caller asked whoever answered the telephone if he or she knew that Jerry Voorhis was a communist and then hung up.

Nixon's ability to tap into people's fears, his careful preparation and hard campaigning, and his deliberate misrepresentations of the truth paid off. Nixon defeated Voorhis in the November election. Voorhis refrained from public comment about the campaign for twenty years. Later, Voorhis recalled that he

> expected that the campaign would be fought around the vital issues of the time as had been the case with all my five previous campaigns. . . . I did not expect my loyalty to America's constitutional government to be attacked. . . . This became the principal refrain of the Nixon cam-

paign, with overtones and undertones questioning my loyalty to American principles. One Nixon campaign leaflet proclaimed that "A vote for Nixon is a vote against the PAC, its Communist principles and its gigantic slush fund."[8]

The campaign confirmed for Nixon that Americans' fears of communism were real. It also confirmed that his campaign tactics worked. He would successfully use these tactics again to gain higher offices.

Richard Nixon, Congressman

Nixon and his wife, Pat, whom he married in 1940, moved from California to Washington, D.C., and became part of the national political scene. Nixon was sworn in as a congressman in January 1947 and was assigned to various House committees that attend to much of the preliminary work on legislation and other matters. Among Nixon's duties was to serve on the House Un-American Activities Committee (HUAC).

Richard Nixon confers with other members of the House Un-American Activities Committee.

HUAC had been established in 1938 to investigate un-American, or traitorous, activities within the United States. Its flamboyant, sometimes irresponsible investigations had quickly given HUAC a bad reputation in Washington. Nixon accepted the assignment with "considerable reluctance" because of this. But he accepted because, like many other Americans, he was becoming more concerned about communism. In his memoirs, he recalled:

> My own attitude toward communism had recently changed from one of general disinterest to one of extreme concern. I do not recall being particularly disturbed when [U.S. President] Roosevelt recognized the Soviet Union in 1934. . . . But as the Communist subjugation of Eastern Europe became more and more apparent—with the takeover of Hungary in 1947 and Czechoslovakia in 1948—I realized that the defeat of Hitler and Japan had not produced a lasting peace, and freedom was now threatened by a new and even more dangerous enemy.[9]

Nixon lost no time establishing himself in Congress as a fervent anticommunist. On February 18, 1947, he made his first speech before the entire House. Instead of the traditional policy statements that freshmen congressmen usually make, Nixon surprised his new colleagues by launching an attack on Gerhart Eisler, a known communist agent who had earlier refused to testify before HUAC. Nixon called for a contempt of Congress citation against Eisler for his refusal to testify. In the House vote on the issue, only one congressman voted against the contempt citation. Eisler was sentenced to a year in prison.

In October 1947, HUAC began an investigation of the film industry in Hollywood, which it considered a hotbed of communist activities. The committee's hearings captured national attention. Ten screenwriters refused to cooperate when confronted by HUAC. As he had in the Eisler case, Nixon delivered a speech on the House floor that won contempt citations for the Hollywood Ten, as the screenwriters were called. They also received jail sentences.

The fate of the Hollywood Ten had repercussions throughout the film industry. Movie studios secretly blacklisted, or shut out, the Hollywood Ten and anyone

When Nixon and the House Un-American Activities Committee began to investigate alleged communists in Hollywood, this group of movie stars flew to Washington, D.C. to protest the action.

Very Intelligent, Tough Men

Nixon described in his memoirs what he learned about communism during a government trip to Europe in 1947. These impressions would influence his stand against communism throughout his career.

"First, the Communist leaders were strong and vigorous: they knew what they wanted and were willing to work hard to get it. After this visit, I would never make the mistake of thinking, either because of the doubletalk party line jargon or because their manners are often crude, that Communist leaders are not very intelligent and very tough men.

Second, I saw how the leaders of postwar European communism understood the power of nationalism and were appropriating that power. While we were in Rome, for example, Communist posters for the upcoming municipal elections were plastered all over the city. These posters did not feature the hammer and sickle, or any other Communist symbol, nor did they depict the joys of some future workers' state. Instead, they were huge heroic pictures of the nineteenth-century patriot Garibaldi—who would have turned over in his grave had he known that his life's devotion to Italy and freedom was being manipulated by an international statist ideology ruled from Moscow.

Third, I saw how European communism was rolling in Soviet money. Unlike most of their democratic counterparts, the European Communist parties were well financed from Moscow.

Fourth, I saw that most of democratic Europe was either leaderless or, worse still, that many in the leadership classes had simply capitulated to communism. For the first time, I understood the vital importance of strong leadership to a people and a nation, and I saw the sad consequences when such leadership is lacking or when it fails. From just this brief exposure, I could see that the only thing the Communists would respect—and deal with seriously—was power at least equal to theirs and backed up by willingness to use it. . . . One basic rule with Russians—never bluff unless you are prepared to carry through, because they will test you every time."

whose political loyalties might fall under suspicion because they feared future action by HUAC. The blacklisting unfairly ruined the careers of many members of the movie industry.

The Alger Hiss Case

In August 1948, HUAC began a new investigation that evolved into what has been called the greatest spy case of the century. In the summer of 1948, HUAC heard testimony about a communist spy ring by a witness named Whittaker Chambers. Chambers was a rumpled, squat man who was an editor with *Time* magazine. He had been a member of the Communist party as a young man but left the party in 1938. Testifying before the committee, Chambers implicated Alger Hiss as a fellow communist, repeating allegations he had first made to other government officials ten years earlier.

Alger Hiss was a prominent Baltimore lawyer who had risen through the ranks of the U.S. State Department during World War II to become a key government official. He served as an aide to President Franklin D. Roosevelt during the 1945 Yalta conference, a meeting of the leaders of the United States, the Soviet Union, and Great Britian. Later, Hiss had chaired the organizing session of the United Nations. Due in part to Chambers's old allegations, Hiss had been investigated by the Federal Bureau of Investigation (FBI), which had been unable to prove Chambers's allegations. Nevertheless, the FBI suggested that Hiss be eased out of government. Hiss left government service and in 1947 became president of the Carnegie

Alger Hiss, a prominent Baltimore lawyer, was investigated by HUAC because he was accused of being a communist spy.

Endowment for International Peace.

Upon hearing about Chambers's HUAC testimony, Alger Hiss demanded that he be allowed to testify before the committee in his own defense. He appeared before HUAC on August 5, 1948. As neat as Chambers was rumpled, Hiss was coolheaded and answered questions confidently. He denied that he knew anyone by the name of Whittaker Chambers and denied all of Chambers's vague allegations. At the conclusion of his testimony, it appeared that Hiss had successfully refuted Chambers's charges.

Meeting privately, the committee members were impressed by the soundness of Hiss's testimony and feared that they had been taken in by Chambers. Some committee members favored dropping the Hiss investigation to spare themselves and HUAC further embarrassment. But Nixon insisted on continuing the investigation. He argued that the case would be dropped by other government agencies that were pursuing separate investigations if the committee did not pursue it. The future of HUAC hinged on the case, he argued, and since Hiss's name had been made public, they were obligated to see the investigation through to its conclusion.

Recalling Hiss's carefully worded answers, Nixon thought the man might be lying. He decided to try to prove that Hiss lied when he claimed not to know Whittaker Chambers. If Hiss could be proved a liar, then his denial of Chambers's other allegations would be called into doubt.

The committee first interviewed Chambers, asking for every detail he could recall about his relationship with Alger Hiss and his wife. Later, Hiss was questioned on the same points. The answers were then compared. The committee found so many similarities in the two testimonies, it concluded that Chambers had indeed known Hiss as he had claimed. That meant that Hiss had lied when he said he did not know Chambers.

The committee arranged a secret confrontation between Hiss and Chambers at New York City's Commodore Hotel. After the two men stood face-to-face, Hiss told the committee that he believed Chambers to be a man he had known as George Crosley. Still, he denied all of Chambers's charges and threatened to sue Chambers if he made those charges outside the legal protection of the committee.

Despite all the testimony, the case seemed to come down to Chambers's word against Hiss's. While the committee was stalled over the case, Hiss filed a libel suit against Chambers. On November 16, 1948, Chambers suddenly produced government documents and notes in Hiss's own handwriting that he claimed Hiss had originally given him ten years before.

Word of the "Baltimore documents," as these papers were called, soon leaked to members of the committee. Later, HUAC subpoenaed all materials Chambers had that were relevant to the Hiss case. When HUAC investigators arrived at Chambers's farm to claim the subpoenaed materials,

HUAC arranged a secret confrontation between Alger Hiss and Whittaker Chambers at New York City's Commodore Hotel.

Richard Nixon (right) examines the Pumpkin Papers which were used as evidence to convict Alger Hiss of perjury.

The Alger Hiss spy case was a pivotal event in American history. While other events, such as the fall of China to communism in 1949, increased fears of the spread of communism throughout the world, the Hiss case convinced Americans that communism also threatened their country from within. In the early 1950s, searching for communists within the U.S. government would become a national obsession.

The Hiss case was a landmark in Nixon's career. Throughout the case, Nixon maneuvered behind the scenes, leaked information to the press, and carefully positioned himself. As a result of his dedication and his political savvy, Nixon became

Hiss, the prisoner on the right, was sentenced to five years in prison for lying under oath.

Chambers led them through the darkness to his garden. There, he took the top off a pumpkin and pulled out a wax paper package containing rolls of microfilm. Chambers also gave the aides copies of the Baltimore documents and other papers.

The Pumpkin Papers created a national sensation and got the Hiss case moving again. Alger Hiss was indicted on two counts of perjury, or lying under oath, on December 15, 1948. He was not charged with spying because the statute of limitations on that charge had expired.

The trial for perjury began in June 1949 and continued into July. The central issue of the trial was Chambers's credibility. The jury could not reach a decision, and the trial ended with a hung jury. In a second trial, Hiss was convicted on both counts of perjury.

Nixon campaigns at a cafe in California for election to the Senate.

nationally famous, an instant hero in the fight against communism. As the years passed and Nixon's political success continued, others involved in breaking the Hiss case gradually slipped from the public eye. Nixon would be remembered as the star of the Alger Hiss case.

But in Nixon's own view, at least, there was a negative side to the Hiss case. Although Nixon had been largely successful in cultivating the national press during the Hiss case, he perceived that the media had turned against him because of his success. In his memoirs, he recalled:

> While there is no doubt that my reputation from the Hiss case launched me on the road to the vice presidency, it also turned me from a relatively popular young congressman, enjoying a good but limited press, into one of the most controversial figures in Washington, bitterly opposed by the most respected and influential liberal journalists and opinion leaders of the time.[10]

For the remainder of his career, Nixon attributed any media attack on him to what he called the vendetta of the liberal press against him for his role in the Hiss case.

From the House to the Senate

Although Nixon had easily won reelection to the House in 1948, the Republican party as a whole had fared badly in the national elections. The Republicans were now the minority party in both the House and Senate. A Democrat, Harry Truman, had been elected president.

Nixon felt that as long as the Republicans remained a minority in the House, he would have little real future there. If his political career were to advance, Nixon felt his future lay in the more prestigious and powerful Senate.

Nixon decided to run for a California seat in the Senate in the 1950 election. Numerous supporters advised him to stay in the House rather than risk defeat in the Senate race. Nixon ignored them. He easily won his party's primary and became the Republican candidate for Senate.

His opponent in the Senate campaign was Congresswoman Helen Gahagan Douglas. Douglas was a Democrat who had served three terms in Congress. She had been an actress before entering politics and was married to popular film star Melvyn Douglas.

Nixon used his 1946 campaign against Jerry Voorhis as a blueprint for his 1950 Senate campaign. Again, he ran an aggressive campaign that focused as much on discrediting Douglas as on issues. He used the same tactics to dominate local California press

The Flaws of Helen Douglas

Nixon recalled in his memoirs how he had to defend his campaign methods in the 1950 Senate race against Helen Gahagan Douglas.

"The 1950 campaign became highly controversial because of the 'rocking, socking' way in which I was said to have waged and won it. Mrs. Douglas and many of her friends and supporters claimed that I had impugned her loyalty and smeared her character, thus depriving the voters of the opportunity to make an honest choice. . . .

Helen Gahagan Douglas waged a campaign that would not be equaled for stridency, ineptness, or self-righteousness until George McGovern's presidential campaign twenty-two years later. In the long run, however, even this probably made little difference. Helen Douglas lost the election because the voters of California in 1950 were not prepared to elect as their senator anyone with a left-wing voting record or anyone they perceived as being soft on or naive about communism. She may have been at some political disadvantage because she was a woman. But her fatal disadvantage lay in her record and in her views."

Nixon's campaign against Helen Gahagan Douglas concentrated as much on discrediting the congresswoman as it did on the issues of the day.

Helen Gahagan Douglas was portrayed as a communist sympathizer in the 1950 senatorial campaign.

coverage, successfully promoting his own candidacy while almost entirely shutting out press coverage for Douglas.

Nixon also again exploited the communist threat in this campaign. While Nixon avoided calling Douglas a communist in public, he attempted to link her to known communists or communist sympathizers and let the public draw the inference for themselves. The Nixon campaign produced an analysis of Douglas's voting record in the House of Representatives that "proved" she had a nearly identical voting record to that of Vito Marcantonio, a left-wing Congressman generally considered to be a communist supporter. The document was printed on pink paper and became known

Nixon Didn't Care How He Won

Helen Gahagan Douglas presented her views of the 1950 Senate race in her autobiography, A Full Life, *published in 1982.*

"When people criticized Nixon for the smear tactics he used against me, he defended himself with a number of justifications. One was that he couldn't avoid making communism an issue because [an earlier campaigner] already had accused me of every red affiliation, short of actually saying that I was a communist. Or he said that he was famous for his involvement in the Alger Hiss case and so was expected to continue to guard America against communists.

Nixon denied that his office made the phone calls about me being a communist. He even claimed for a time that such calls never happened. Faced with irrefutable proof that they did, he declared that my supporters had placed the calls in order to create an issue! . . .

There's not much to say about the 1950 campaign except that a man ran for Senate who wanted to get there, and didn't care how."

Nixon congratulates himself on his electoral lead over Helen Gahagan Douglas in the Senate race of 1950.

as the Pink Sheet. The color carried a subtle message. *Pinko* was a term used to describe individuals who were sympathetic to the cause of communists, or Reds.

The accuracy of the Pink Sheet was later discredited. But with it and other "dirty" campaign tactics, Nixon succeeded in keeping the Douglas campaign on the defensive. Douglas denied Nixon's charges and claimed that Nixon was using unfair campaign practices. She called him Tricky Dick because of the Pink Sheet and his other dirty campaign tricks. It was a nickname that would stay with Nixon through the rest of his career.

Nixon turned Douglas's defenses around and called them smears against his character. His organization's dominance of the press was so effective that often Douglas's charges against him were never printed, but his responses to them were.

As in 1946, Nixon volunteers made nearly half a million phone calls throughout California. In each call, the campaign worker asked whoever answered if he or she knew that Helen Douglas was a communist and then hung up. Like Jerry Voorhis, Helen Gahagan Douglas proved no match for the ingenious methods of the Nixon organization. Nixon won election to the U.S. Senate by a wide margin.

Both candidates later recalled the 1950 election in their memoirs. Nixon remembered the Douglas campaign for its "ineptness" and denied charges that he had "impugned her loyalty and smeared her character." Douglas's "fatal disadvantage lay in her record and in her views," Nixon insisted. Douglas would remember the campaign differently. "There's not much to say about the 1950 campaign," she wrote, "except that a man ran for Senate who wanted to get there and didn't care how."

Nixon had employed numerous "dirty tricks" in his successful campaigns for the House and Senate. These dirty tricks remained hidden from the public for many years. But two decades later, dirty tricks would reemerge as a major theme in his career and lead to his downfall.

3 Toward the Vice-Presidency

Nixon's election to the Senate took him one step closer to his ultimate goal of the presidency. Almost immediately, he began positioning himself to take his next step—to become the 1952 Republican candidate for vice-president.

Political parties officially nominate their presidential and vice-presidential candidates at a national convention the summer before the election. In the months preceding the convention, however, candidates from both parties campaign to win a series of smaller elections called primaries, in which voters from each party decide who they prefer to represent them. In this way,

candidates win enough delegate support to secure their nomination at the convention.

There were several strong presidential candidates within the Republican party in 1952. Among them was Gen. Dwight D. Eisenhower. Although not a professional politician, Eisenhower had been the supreme commander of the Western allies during World War II and was well known and respected in the United States and in Europe. After the war, he had served as president of Columbia University and later returned to Europe as commander of the North Atlantic Treaty Organization (NATO) forces.

Gen. Dwight D. Eisenhower was the Republican presidential candidate in the 1952 presidential election.

The Republican party nominated Eisenhower and Nixon for president and vice-president at the national convention in 1952.

To Eisenhower's campaign organizers, Nixon seemed like an ideal running mate. Nixon's role in the Alger Hiss case had made him nationally famous and established him as a leader in the anticommunist movement. He was knowledgeable in international affairs. Nixon's youth complemented Eisenhower's mature, almost fatherly image. Most important, Nixon was from California, now the nation's second most populous state. This could help Eisenhower win in California, a state considered critical in securing both the nomination and the election.

Eisenhower and Nixon were nominated at the Republican party's national convention in Chicago in July 1952. Nixon had played a major role in helping Eisenhower win the nomination. His performance at the convention demonstrated that he was a master politician. Nixon would remain a central figure in the Republican party for the next two decades.

The two candidates had little time to savor their nomination victory, however. Almost before the campaign started, a scandal erupted around Richard Nixon that threatened not only his candidacy but his entire political career.

The Fund Crisis

On September 14, 1952, as the campaign was getting into full swing, Nixon was asked by a reporter about a secret fund. The secret fund had been created by members of Nixon's staff to finance some of Nixon's expenses as a senator. At the time it became an issue, the balance of the fund totaled approximately eighteen thousand dollars.

Nixon acknowledged the fund's existence and referred further questions about it to a member of his staff. No one suspected that this simple exchange would touch off a crisis that would make history.

The secret fund became public knowledge on September 18, 1952, when articles describing it in detail were published in several national newspapers. The articles raised immediate concern about Nixon's ethics. Existence of the fund made people fear that Nixon had been "bought" by those who had contributed to the fund. People wondered if he had repaid his contributors with political favors.

Nixon was just beginning a whistle-stop campaign trip aboard a train called

The Fund Crisis

In covering the Fund Crisis in Nixon's 1952 campaign for vice-president of the United States, the press offered differing views about his conduct.

"There are legal ways and customary ways by which members of Congress augment their official income, and there are illegal ways. Senator Nixon has chosen the most open and straightforward of all legal ways to do so, and stands entirely ready to make any accounting his accusers want. One additional remark should be made about the attack on Senator Nixon. It came from James Wechsler and the *New York Post*. Mr. Wechsler was a Washington correspondent before he became managing editor of The *Post*. He knows quite well there is nothing unusual or questionable about what Senator Nixon has done." (*Minneapolis Star*)

"People begin wondering whether a man who kicks in a few hundred bucks to help a lawmaker make clerical ends meet might not ask a favor in return. And even if the favor is never asked, the lawmaker has no business accepting such money, however noble the ends he seeks. He [Nixon] has hurt the campaign of his thoroughly honorable superior, General Eisenhower." (*Pittsburgh Post Gazette*)

Nixon addresses a question during the 1952 vice-presidential campaign.

"It is with the deepest sense of disappointment that this newspaper . . . asks Senator Nixon to resign his candidacy. It seems unimportant the gifts were made to some sort of special fund. The money was constructively available to Senator Nixon, to be spent on his say so, and the damning point is that it was given to him after his election, and not before his election, when he faced an expensive campaign. . . . But post-campaign gifts, no matter how honorably they are received and how properly they are spent, inevitably must smack of the greased palm, the bought politician. . . . Senator Nixon's record so far as we are advised is one of unimpeachable devotion to the public interest. But his acceptance of these post-election gifts cannot be explained away." (*The New York Times*)

In his home town of Whittier, California, Nixon appears in a local parade to campaign for vice-president.

the *Nixon Special* when the fund story broke. Asked about the articles late that night, Nixon dismissed them as part of the smear campaign directed at him by the liberal press as a result of his role in the Alger Hiss case.

The next day, as his train was pulling away from a campaign stop, a heckler shouted, "Tell us about the $16,000!" misquoting the actual amount in the fund. Nixon ordered the train to a halt. Speaking spontaneously, he again labeled the story a "smear" and claimed that he was actually saving the taxpayers money by using the fund. He noted that his wife was not on his payroll, but John Sparkman, the vice-presidential candidate in the Democratic party, had his wife on the payroll. Nixon implied that such a practice was immoral. He vowed to continue the campaign despite the smears. Nixon's impromptu speech dodged the real issue of the fund's legality and shifted the focus to his opponent's credibility. The crowd cheered him. At succeeding stops, Nixon honed his defense.

Half a continent away, Eisenhower's own campaign train was beginning a trip through the Midwest. The ethical issue raised by the existence of the fund was particularly embarrassing to Eisenhower because a central theme of his campaign trip was to end corruption in politics.

The fund issue caused tremendous tension between Nixon and Eisenhower. The two candidates stopped talking to one another, although their aides worked diligently via telephone to find a solution to the crisis. Nixon did not want to resign but felt that the decision was Eisenhower's to make. Eisenhower wavered between supporting Nixon and calling for him to step down.

While campaign workers for Nixon and Eisenhower searched for a solution, the fund issue was debated by the press. Some newspapers defended Nixon. Others questioned his judgment or concluded that he had hurt the campaign. Some newspapers called for his resignation. Taking a middle-of-the-road position, the *Philadelphia Inquirer* called upon Nixon to account for himself:

> The disclosure is a serious matter that demands explanation. Attempts made by some of Nixon's friends to fasten the label of "Communist smear" upon

reports of the fund miss the point entirely. The question is this: Was it right or wrong for him to accept these contributions? Senator Nixon may have a wholly acceptable explanation—with details, not generalities—showing that there was nothing improper or unethical about any part of the transaction. He should produce it at once.[11]

Early on Sunday morning, September 21, Nixon decided to appeal to the American public. His defense of the fund during his train's campaign stops had been well received by the audiences. He decided to present his side of the story on national television and let the people decide for themselves. It was the biggest risk he had taken in his political career. If the American public reacted negatively, Nixon would have little choice but to step down as the vice-presidential candidate. If, however, the public responded favorably, it would make it more difficult for Eisenhower to remove him from the ticket. Nixon and Eisenhower spoke by telephone late that evening about Nixon's plan. Eisenhower agreed that Nixon should go on television, but no decision was made about the future of his candidacy.

The speech was scheduled for Tuesday evening, September 23. For the next two days, calls for Nixon's resignation increased in the press. In the afternoon before his speech, Nixon received some good news about the fund. A law firm and an accounting firm hired to review the fund's finances issued reports stating that the fund was not illegal and that none of the funds had gone to Nixon for personal use.

A short time before he was to go before the cameras, however, Nixon received a tremendous blow from Eisenhower. He was informed by aides that Eisenhower suggested that he resign at the end of his speech. Shaken and angry, Nixon went on television. Throughout the United States, sixty million people gathered around television sets. This was the largest audience in history to witness a political speech.

Nixon began by telling the television audience that accepting the eighteen thousand dollars in contributions would be morally wrong if he had taken the money for personal use, if he had taken it secretly, or if contributors received "special favors" for their contributions. He then declared:

> Not one cent of the $18,000 or any other money of that type ever went to me for my personal use. . . . It was not a secret fund. . . . And third, let me point out, and I want to make this

Nixon and his family pose with their dog, Checkers. During the Fund Crisis, the dog was the only gift that Nixon admitted receiving.

particularly clear, that no contributor to this fund, no contributor to any of my campaign, has ever received any consideration that he would not have received as an ordinary constituent.[12]

Nixon told the audience that accepting the contributions was the only way that he could "handle necessary political expenses of getting my message to the American people." He cited the independent reports by the law firm and the accounting firm that concluded he had not violated the law by accepting the contributions. To prove that he was telling the truth, Nixon then presented his complete financial history. He admitted that he had accepted one gift, a black-and-white cocker spaniel named Checkers "that regardless of what they say about it, we're gonna keep it."

Nixon then brilliantly turned the crisis into an opportunity to campaign in front

Not a Secret Fund

Richard Nixon defended himself on national television on September 23, 1952, during the Fund Crisis and told the sixty million people watching that he was innocent.

"Not one cent of the $18,000 or any other money of that type ever went for my personal use. Every penny of it was used to pay for political expenses that I did not think should be charged to the taxpayers of the United States.

It was not a secret fund. As a matter of fact, when I was on 'Meet the Press,' . . . Peter Edson came up to me after the program and he said, 'Dick, what about this fund we hear about?' And I said, Well, there's no secret about it. Go out and see Dana Smith, who was the administrator of the fund. And I gave him his address, and I said that you will find that the purpose of the fund simply was to defray political expenses that I did not feel should be charged to the Government.

And third, let me point out, and I want to make this particularly clear, that no contributor to this fund, no contributor to any of my campaign, has ever received any consideration that he would not have received as an ordinary constituent.

I just don't believe in that and I can say that never, while I have been in the Senate of the United States, as far as the people that contributed to this fund are concerned, have I made a telephone call for them to an agency, or have I gone down to an agency in their behalf. And the record will show that."

A Magnificent Presentation

After Nixon's speech, Republican presidential candidate Dwight Eisenhower sent Nixon a congratulatory telegram in which he requested a meeting. The telegram was published in the September 24, 1952, New York Times.

"Your presentation was magnificent. While technically no decision rests with me, yet you and I know that the realities of the situation will require a personal pronouncement, which so far as the public is concerned will be considered decisive.

In view of your comprehensive presentation my personal decision is going to be based on a personal conclusion. To complete the formulation of that personal decision I feel the need for talking to you and would be most appreciative if you could fly to see me at once. Tomorrow evening I shall be in Wheeling, West Virginia. I cannot close the telegram without saying that whatever personal admiration and affection I have for you, and they are great, are undiminished."

---

of sixty million people. He called attention to a similar fund belonging to Adlai Stevenson, the Democratic candidate for president, and suggested that Stevenson and his running mate, John Sparkman, make similar financial disclosures. Shifting gears, he vowed to continue the fight despite the "smears" made against him. He cited the communist threat and declared that General Eisenhower was the only candidate who could "rid the Government of both those who are Communists and those who have corrupted this Government."

Instead of resigning, he submitted "to the Republican National Committee . . . the decision which is theirs to make." He urged listeners to wire their feelings to that committee and concluded by calling Eisenhower a great man.

The speech contained various falsehoods, large and small. The fund *had* been

secret prior to the crisis. The speech also addressed only those issues that had been raised by the press. Nixon's financial backing actually went much deeper than what was reported by the media and documented by the accounting firm's hurriedly conducted audit. Years later, researchers would document strong connections between Nixon's contributors and his political record, casting much doubt on his claim that he had never granted special consideration to contributors.

Nixon's speech, popularly known as the Checkers speech because of the reference to the family's dog, ranks as one of the most important speeches in modern American history. The overwhelming success of the speech demonstrated to Nixon and other politicians that television could be a powerful ally. Politics was never the same again. In retrospect, the speech revealed much about

Nixon himself. Despite its deliberate lies, it was brilliantly conceived and executed. It showcased Nixon's ability to turn the gravest crisis into a political triumph, a skill he would demonstrate many times in the future. The speech also showed that Nixon would do anything that was necessary to achieve his goals—even endure the humiliation of detailing his personal finances on national television.

The Checkers speech also marked a turning point in the Fund Crisis. Eisenhower immediately wired his congratulations, which were lost amid a blizzard of supportive telegrams from the American public. Eisenhower, however, delayed making a final decision about keeping Nixon on the ticket until after they could meet. He requested that Nixon fly east for a

Despite the Fund Crisis, Eisenhower chose to keep Richard Nixon as his running mate, and the two were elected in 1952.

A Modern-Day Lincoln

Roger Morris in his study of Nixon's early career, Richard Milhous Nixon: The Rise of an American Politician, *describes the overwhelming public response to Nixon's televised defense of his fund.*

"The nation was responding to his speech by historic proportions. As many as four million telegrams, letters, cards, and calls came cascading [in]. . . . There were messages from throughout the forty-eight states, Alaska, Hawaii, and Puerto Rico, from Canada, Americans abroad, ships at sea. Overwhelmingly, it was favorable, by one study as much as seventy-five to one in favor of keeping him on the ticket, and full of accolades—'a deserving man,' 'a big man,' 'a great man,' 'a modern-day Lincoln.'. . . One analysis of over 300,000 telegrams and letters revealed that only 7 percent made any reference to . . . substantive issues. Most of all, they had responded to Nixon himself. For a single dramatic half hour in the autumn of 1952 . . . Richard Nixon had become the quintessential American politician."

President Eisenhower and Vice-President Nixon, at the inaugural parade.

meeting. Nixon was furious. He dictated a resignation telegram to Eisenhower, but an aide immediately tore it up. Nixon defied Eisenhower's request and continued his own campaign trip. Back on the campaign trail, he found that he was more popular than ever.

Nixon and Eisenhower finally met a few days later. After the meeting, Eisenhower formally announced that Nixon would remain on the Republican ticket. But the Fund Crisis permanently scarred the relationship between the two men. Neither ever completely trusted the other again.

In November, the American public showed that Nixon had not only saved his candidacy but had saved his career as well. They elected Richard Nixon vice-president of the United States. He was inaugurated on January 20, 1953.

The election of Nixon to the vice-presidency indicated that the Fund Crisis had not hurt him in the short run. But like other significant themes of his early career, controversies about a secret fund and his personal finances would return to haunt him again. Two decades after his famous Checkers speech, the disclosure of a different secret fund once again hurled Nixon into the center of a controversy that had an even more dramatic impact on his career.

4 Richard Nixon, Vice-President

Being vice-president of the United States is "the easiest job in the world," joked Charles G. Dawes, who served as vice-president under Calvin Coolidge. Dawes claimed that he "had only two responsibilities—to sit and listen to United States senators give speeches, and to check the morning newspapers as to the president's health."

Vice-President Nixon soon came to appreciate the wisdom behind Dawes's joke. Throughout his years as vice-president, Nixon struggled to expand his role beyond ceremonial duties. He found Dawes's comment about the president's health particularly appropriate. The health of President Eisenhower played a key role in the development of Nixon's political career.

Nixon and McCarthy

When Eisenhower took office, all of Washington was being held hostage by one man who, in the guise of fighting communism, had nearly paralyzed the government. He was Senator Joseph McCarthy from Wisconsin. Nixon had unintentionally helped pave the way for McCarthy's swift rise to power. As vice-president, Nixon also played a role in McCarthy's fall.

McCarthy made reckless accusations against government officials, calling them communists or tools of the communist conspiracy. All of Washington cowered before McCarthy. To oppose him was to invite accusations that could destroy a career. McCarthy was afraid of no one.

As long as McCarthy attacked Democrats, he was, in effect, an asset to the

Senator Joseph McCarthy almost halted government operations by recklessly accusing government officials of communism.

Republican party. McCarthy, however, boldly expanded his attacks to include the new Eisenhower administration. He even branded President Eisenhower a traitor.

With these attacks, McCarthy became an embarrassment and a liability to the Republican party. Eisenhower designated Nixon to make the Republican party's response to a speech by Democrat Adlai Stevenson in which he criticized the Eisenhower administration's link to McCarthy. It was an assignment, Nixon wrote in his memoirs, that he accepted with reluctance. He recalled:

My own feelings about Joe McCarthy were mixed. I never shared the disdain with which fashionable Washington treated him. . . . In fact, I found him personally likable, if irresponsibly impulsive. At the end, I felt sorry for him as a man whose zeal and thirst for publicity were leading him and others to destruction. . . . I broke with McCarthy when he began to attack the administration openly. . . . McCarthy was sincere, and I know from personal investigation that there was real substance to some of his charges. But he could not resist grossly exaggerating his facts. The communists and the compulsive anti-communists, together with many who were as anti-communist as McCarthy himself, ended up discrediting everything the man had to say when McCarthy became the issue instead of communism.[13]

Nixon's speech on March 13, 1954, distanced the administration from McCarthy. It

A Bunch of Rats

On March 13, 1954, Vice-President Nixon made a speech that distanced the Eisenhower administration from Senator Joseph McCarthy, without specifically mentioning McCarthy by name. The speech signaled the beginning of the end of McCarthyism. This excerpt from the speech is taken from Nixon's memoirs.

"Now, I can imagine some of you will say, 'Why all this hullabaloo about being fair when you are dealing with a gang of traitors?' As a matter of fact, I heard people say 'After all, we are dealing with a bunch of rats. What we ought to do is go out and shoot them.'

Well, I agree they are a bunch of rats. But just remember this. When you go out to shoot rats, you have to shoot straight, because when you shoot wildly, it not only means that the rats may get away more easily—but you make it easier on the rats. Also you might hit someone else who is trying to shoot rats, too. So, we have to be fair—for two very good reasons: one, because it is right, and two, because it is the most effective way of doing the job."

marked the beginning of the end of McCarthyism in the United States. Behind the scenes, Nixon arranged for the release of a report from the U.S. Army to members of the Senate. The report documented forty-four attempts made by McCarthy and one of his staff members, Roy Cohn, to gain special treatment for army private David Schine, another member of McCarthy's staff.

On December 2, 1954, McCarthy became only the sixth senator in history to be censured, or condemned, by his colleagues in the Senate. After his censure, McCarthy faded from the public spotlight. His aide, Roy Cohn, later stated that McCarthy felt that he had been betrayed by Nixon, whom he had considered a friend. McCarthy descended into alcoholism and died in 1957.

Nixon and Eisenhower

Nixon found the job of being Eisenhower's vice-president frustrating. On the surface, the relationship between the two men was almost affectionate, like that of a father and son. Underneath, however, it was often strained. Part of the tension was a result of their distinctly different political styles. Nixon almost relished controversy and frequently spoke out on issues. His views often generated scorn and ridicule from his critics. He was a regular target of biting political cartoons drawn by popular cartoonist Herbert Lawrence Block—Herblock to his fans.

The controversial Nixon often found himself out of favor with Eisenhower. As an army general, Eisenhower was used to commanding respect and delegating unpleasant matters to his subordinates. He avoided controversy and confrontation with his staff. He addressed problems indirectly, often dropping subtle hints for others to act upon.

Nixon soon discovered that Eisenhower was both the key and the obstacle to his career advancement. Nixon believed that as long as he and Eisenhower were a team, Eisenhower would leave the thankless and sometimes distasteful role of the Republican party "tough guy" to him.

Nixon played the tough guy throughout the election campaign of 1954. Although not up for reelection himself, Nixon campaigned

Despite the outward display of affection between Nixon and Eisenhower, their different political styles often clashed in private.

While President Eisenhower recovered from a heart attack, Nixon served as acting president.

around the country for the Republican candidates running for Congress. As the campaign season progressed, Nixon began to feel the toll public life was taking on him and his wife and two daughters. His memoirs describe how he had tired of politics.

> Although the fund crisis had thickened my skin, I still resented being portrayed as a demagogue or a liar or as the sewer-dwelling denizen of Herblock cartoons in the *Washington Post*. As the attacks became more personal, I sometimes wondered where party loyalty left off and masochism began. The girls were reaching an impressionable age, and neither Pat nor I wanted their father to become the perennial bad guy of American politics.[14]

Just before the 1954 election, Nixon "decided not to run [for vice-president] again in 1956, unless exceptional circumstances intervened to change my mind." He told an aide on Election Day, "I am

through with politics." Others suggest that Nixon's fear that Eisenhower might replace him with a less controversial running mate for the 1956 election was also a factor in his decision.

On the evening of September 24, 1955, Nixon received a telephone call that ultimately changed his mind about retiring from politics. President Eisenhower had suffered a heart attack. Eisenhower's illness was a national crisis (and a personal crisis for Nixon, who cared deeply for Eisenhower, despite their differences). It was also a political opportunity for Nixon. If Eisenhower died, Nixon would immediately succeed him as president and could run for reelection in 1956. Even if Eisenhower recovered fully, he might not run for reelection in 1956, which meant the Republican party would have to pick a new candidate. Nixon would surely be considered for the nomination.

While Eisenhower recovered, Nixon functioned as acting president. He presided over meetings at the White House. He chaired regular meetings of the cabinet and the National Security Council. He signed ceremonial documents on behalf of the president.

Eisenhower returned to Washington only forty-eight days after his heart attack. On the day after Christmas, Eisenhower called Nixon into the Oval Office. Privately, he had concluded that the controversial Nixon had not "grown" enough to be president. Early preference polls had also indicated that voters might prefer another vice-presidential candidate over Nixon. Rather than confront Nixon, Eisenhower suggested that Nixon consider not running for vice-president in 1956 and instead accept a cabinet post. Such a position, Eisenhower said, would give Nixon important administrative experience that the vice-presidency could not provide.

Nixon was thunderstruck. Immediately, he recognized the suggestion as Eisenhower's subtle way of trying to remove him from the ticket. In his memoirs, Nixon charitably attributed responsibility for the suggestion to Eisenhower's aides rather than to the president himself, but he was terribly hurt by the suggestion. A few weeks later, Eisenhower made the suggestion again in a telephone conversation. Nixon later commented that he felt as though the clock had been turned back to the 1952 Fund Crisis. He made no reply, and Eisenhower let the matter drop. What little doubt Nixon might have had about Eisenhower's intentions was erased when one of the president's aides bluntly told Nixon that Eisenhower wanted him off the ticket.

Publicly, Eisenhower evaded the issue of whether he would keep Nixon. He formally announced he would run for reelection on February 29, 1956. When asked if Nixon would be his running mate, he dodged the question by saying it was the national convention's responsibility to select the party's vice-presidential candidate. In a press conference on March 7, Eisenhower only weakly defended Nixon when asked about rumors that he wanted to replace Nixon as his running mate. He told reporters that he would not presume "to tell the Vice President what he should do with his own future." He had only asked Nixon "to chart out his own course."

Many emotions ran through Nixon's mind. He was angered by Eisenhower's maneuvering. He wrote in his memoirs that he did not have "a burning desire to be Vice President." He considered issuing a statement that he would not seek reelection but was persuaded by a colleague to delay his announcement. Despite these feelings, Nixon recognized that remaining on the ticket in 1956 represented his best chance of becoming president of the United States.

If Nixon had many critics, he also had many supporters. Right-wing members of the Republican party rallied to support Nixon's efforts to stay on the ticket. They organized a voluntary write-in vote in the New Hampshire primary election. Nearly half of the fifty-six thousand people who voted for Eisenhower also wrote in Nixon's name as a gesture of support.

In a news conference on April 25, Eisenhower acknowledged the popular support for Nixon. Eisenhower declared that he would "be happy to be on any political ticket in which I was a candidate with [Nixon]." When asked if Vice-President Nixon had "charted his own course," Eisenhower said

After Nixon's political maneuvering garnered electoral support, Eisenhower accepted him as his running mate for the second time.

that Nixon had not reported back to him. This exchange spurred Nixon to action, which he recorded in his memoirs.

Early the next morning, April 26, I called the White House and said that I would like to see the President. That afternoon I sat across the desk from him in the Oval Office. "Mr. President," I said, "I would be honored to continue as Vice President under you. The only reason I waited this long to tell you was that I didn't want to do anything that would make you think I was trying to force my way onto the ticket if you didn't want me on it."[15]

Eisenhower called in an aide and told him that Nixon had just announced he would stay on the ticket. He directed the aide to take Nixon out so that the vice-president could make the announcement to the reporters himself. "And," he added, "you can tell them that I am delighted with the news." The fact that Eisenhower would not make the announcement himself was a humiliating slight to Nixon.

The meeting, however, did not guarantee Nixon's spot on the ticket. On June 8, 1956, Eisenhower had surgery for a partially obstructed lower bowel. The operation rekindled fears that Eisenhower would be unable to complete his first term or run for reelection and spawned a final plan to replace Nixon with a more popular candidate.

Shortly before the convention, Harold Stassen, a prominent figure in the Eisenhower administration, commissioned a private poll that concluded Nixon would lose more votes than any other vice-presidential candidate. Stassen met with Eisenhower and offered to lead a movement to replace Nixon with another candidate.

Nixon discusses Eisenhower's health with reporters.

Eisenhower, who had recovered quickly from his operation, declined to take part in the movement but did nothing to stop it. Nixon and his supporters easily outmaneuvered Stassen, and the plan fell apart. But the fact that Eisenhower had not immediately rejected Stassen's plan further angered and hurt Nixon.

Eisenhower and Nixon were renominated at the Republican national convention on August 22, 1956. In November, they easily defeated the Democratic candidate, Adlai Stevenson. Their second term as president and vice-president of the United States began in January 1957.

On November 25, 1957, only eleven months into his second term, Eisenhower suffered a stroke. Nixon again faced the possibility that he would become president. Eisenhower, however, returned to Washington only four days after his stroke. He resumed a limited schedule immediately and within a short time, resumed a complete schedule. Eisenhower completed his term without further illness.

Nixon is sworn in to his second term as vice-president of the United States.

The complicated relationship between Nixon and Eisenhower continued throughout their second term. The two men had obvious affection for each other but never overcame their differences. Nixon remained bewildered and hurt by Eisenhower's aloofness and angered by his efforts to replace him in 1956. Eisenhower, on the other hand, seemed to remain perpetually disappointed with Nixon.

Journey to South America

Despite their complicated relationship, Eisenhower and Nixon continued to work together. In the spring of 1958, Nixon made a goodwill trip to South America at Eisenhower's insistence. The purpose of the trip was to attend the inauguration of Arturo Frondizi, the newly elected president of Argentina. Eisenhower hoped Nixon's attendance would dispel the impression that the United States had supported the hated Argentine dictator Juan Peron. The trip was soon expanded to include several other South American countries.

Nixon was not eager to go and expected the trip to be so routine that he advised reporters not to bother accompanying him. In some respects, Nixon was not the best choice of a goodwill ambassador. As a strong anticommunist, he had made statements in support of brutal South American dictators just because these men were also anticommunist.

Had Nixon confined his activities to ceremonial duties, his trip might have

In Lima, Peru, demonstrators confront Nixon in front of San Marcos University.

Angry crowds threw rocks through the windows of the cars in Nixon's motorcade during his visit to Venezuela.

remained routine. But he could not resist the opportunity to generate publicity. He mingled with the crowds that lined the streets along which his motorcade passed. In Uruguay, Argentina, Paraguay, and Bolivia, Nixon was greeted warmly. A crush of people surrounded him in Argentina, preventing him from attending the inauguration, which was the original purpose of his trip.

In Lima, Peru, Nixon was confronted by demonstrators at San Marcos University who chanted "Death to Nixon" and other slogans. When Nixon confronted them, they threw rocks and other objects at him. Nixon was grazed by a rock. He insulted the crowd by calling them cowards and kicked one demonstrator in the shins. Later in the visit, Nixon and his wife were spat upon by demonstrators.

The trip continued through Ecuador and Colombia without incident. In Caracas, Venezuela, crowds were again hostile. Nixon's motorcade was halted by demonstrators. Nixon recalled the moment in his memoirs:

We realized that we were completely alone as the first rock hit the car window, lodging itself in the glass and spraying us with tiny slivers. One sliver hit the Foreign Minister in the eye, and he started to bleed heavily. He tried to stop the blood, moaning over and over, "This is terrible. This is terrible."

I saw a thug with an iron pipe work his way up to the car. He was looking right at me as he began trying to break the window. . . . Suddenly the car began to move, and the idea that we had somehow broken free gave me a surge of relief. Then I realized that the crowd was rocking the car back and forth—slower and higher each time. I remembered that it was a common tactic for mobs to turn a car over and then set it on fire. . . . I believe that at that moment, for the first time, each of us in the car realized we might actually be killed.[16]

At one point during the crisis, Secret Service agents riding with the vice-president drew their guns, but Nixon wisely ordered

Not a Triumph

The May 15, 1958, edition of the New York Times *commented on Vice-President Nixon's ill-fated "goodwill trip" to South America.*

"The capital will turn out tomorrow to give Vice President Richard M. Nixon a triumphant 'welcome home' from his trip to eight Latin American countries.

The plan for the gala welcome for the Vice President and Mrs. Nixon grew almost spontaneously today as a demonstration of national unity and purpose after the indignities they have suffered, culminating in yesterday's mob attack in Caracas, Venezuela. . . .

Despite the welcome for the Vice President, there was a realization in Washington today that his trip, planned as a "goodwill" tour, had not been a triumph for United States policy south of the border. . . . There was no disposition here to criticize Mr. Nixon; in fact there was nothing but praise for the way he had comported himself under the most trying circumstances.

In Congress, expressions of shock and anger at the treatment accorded to Mr. Nixon were interspersed with remarks betraying deep concern over United States policy and demands for a re-evaluation of that policy."

Nixon and his wife ride home with President Eisenhower after Nixon's unpopular trip to South America.

them to put the weapons away. The local police finally intervened, and the motorcade made its way to the safety of the American Embassy.

Communication lines between the United States and Caracas had become garbled. Eisenhower received messages that the city of Caracas was out of control and that the vice-president was in grave danger. Eisenhower put troops on alert and sent ships steaming toward Venezuela to stage a rescue. When he heard about Eisenhower's actions, Nixon was appalled. The crisis was already over and he knew that the maneuver would be misinterpreted. The rescue effort was called off.

As a goodwill mission, the trip was a disaster. To save face, the Eisenhower administration gave Nixon a hero's welcome upon his return to Washington. Eisenhower himself, members of his cabinet, and congressmen met Nixon's plane. The publicity and the hero's welcome temporarily boosted Nixon's popularity at home. He ranked even with the Democratic candidates in the early polls for the 1960 presidential election.

Debating Khrushchev

Throughout the 1950s, the cold war between the United States and the Soviet Union had continued on many fronts. The leaders of each country genuinely feared nuclear attack from the other. For a decade, each country had struggled to contain the other's influence throughout the world. American and Soviet citizens mistrusted each other.

Despite this hostile atmosphere, the two governments made attempts to learn more about each other. Early in 1959, the Soviet Union sponsored a science exhibition in New York, and Vice-President Nixon spoke at its opening. The United States sponsored an American Exhibition in Moscow later that year. The exhibition

Eisenhower arranged a hero's welcome for Nixon to save face after the vice-president's humiliating South American tour.

presented Nixon with an opportunity to go to Moscow and meet with Nikita Khrushchev, the leader of the Communist party in the Soviet Union. Nixon knew that the meeting would provide him with further experience he could use in his quest to become president. Nixon diligently prepared for the trip, mastering the answers to more than one hundred questions that Khrushchev might ask him.

There were several meetings between Nixon and Khrushchev, but it was a spontaneous debate in the kitchen of a "typical American home" on display in the exhibition

---

Threats

On August 3, 1959, Newsweek *magazine published portions of the famous Kitchen Debate between Vice-President Nixon and Premier Nikita Khrushchev of the Soviet Union. In their debate, the two leaders articulated the differences between the United States and the Soviet Union.*

Nixon: "We are both strong. . . . Neither should use that strength to put the other in a position where he in effect has an ultimatum. . . . With modern weapons it does not make any difference [who is stronger] if war comes. We both have had it."

Khrushchev (*sounding surprised*): " . . . If all Americans agree with you, then whom don't we agree with?"

Nixon (*pushing the point*): "I hope the Prime Minister has understood all the implications of what I have just said. . . . When we sit down at a conference table it cannot be all one way. One side cannot put an ultimatum to the other. It is impossible."

Khrushchev (*flushing red*): "Who is giving an ultimatum? We know something about politics too. Let your correspondents compare stop watches and see who is filibustering. You put great emphasis on diktat [handing down decrees]. Our country has never been guided by diktat."

Nixon: "I'm talking about it in the international sense."

Khrushchev: "It sounds to me like a threat. We too are giants. You want to threaten—we will answer threats with threats."

Nixon: "That's not my point. We will never engage in threats."

Khrushchev: ". . . We have the means to threaten too. . . . Ours are better. . . ."

Nixon: ". . . I don't think that the cause of peace is helped by reminders that you have greater strength than we because that is a threat too."

Nixon speaks during the spontaneous "Kitchen Debate" with Krushchev in the Moscow exhibition of a "typical American home."

that Americans remembered most. A debate between Nixon and Khrushchev on utensils in American and Soviet kitchens quickly turned into a confrontation over weapons technology. For several exciting moments, the two men sparred verbally, each accusing the other of threatening world peace. The confrontation ended just as quickly as it began, with appeals for peace by both leaders. Transcripts of the exchange that were printed in the American press portrayed Nixon as the peacemaker and clearly showed that he had kept a cooler head than the fiery Khrushchev.

The confrontation had little or no effect on the relationship between the two countries. But it did give Nixon valuable publicity. He appeared on the cover of *Life* magazine and was praised in *Time* and *Newsweek* for his excellent performance.

The favorable publicity Nixon received as the man who stood up to Khrushchev and communism could not have come at a better time. In little more than a year, Eisenhower would be leaving the White House after completing his second term. The Republican party would choose a new candidate for president, and Richard Nixon was now a front-runner for the nomination.

5 Running for President

In 1960, Nixon formally began the quest he had been preparing for since he was a boy. He declared himself a candidate for the Republican party's nomination for president. Nixon was clearly the front-runner for the nomination. His major competition came from New York governor Nelson Rockefeller. Nixon appealed to conservative and moderate members of the party, while Rockefeller appealed to the party liberals. Throughout the series of primary elections, Nixon maintained a solid lead over Rockefeller. Rockefeller concluded that he could not win the nomination, so he turned his attention toward having his views built into the Republican party's platform, which is the party's statement of its position on important campaign issues. A few days before the convention was to begin, Rockefeller threatened to lead a fight on the floor against adoption of the platform that had already been drafted by a committee.

Nixon wanted to avoid an open split between the conservative and liberal wings of the party. Without informing his campaign staff, Nixon flew to New York and met personally with Rockefeller in his apartment on Fifth Avenue. The two men redrafted the civil rights and national defense planks of the platform to reflect Rockefeller's more liberal views. The agreement, known as the Compact of Fifth

Avenue, was termed a "sellout" by Nixon supporters, although the new planks were not radically different from those they replaced. In compromising, Nixon accomplished his goal of unifying the party behind him.

At the convention, Nixon easily won the nomination for president. During the meeting that produced the Compact of Fifth Avenue, Nixon had offered Rockefeller the vice-presidential nomination, which Rockefeller declined. Nixon later wrote that he was not especially disappointed when Rockefeller

Nixon campaigns for the presidency in Oregon.

The President's Burden

In a radio speech on September 19, 1968, Nixon explained the nature of the presidency and why he wanted to pursue the office.

"The answer is not one of glory, or fame; today the burdens of the office outweigh its privileges. It's not because the Presidency offers a chance to *be* somebody, but because it offers a chance to *do* something. . . .

We stand at a great turning point—when the nation is groping for a new direction, unsure of its role and its purposes, caught in a tumult of change. And for the first time, we face serious, simultaneous threats to the peace both at home and abroad.

In the watershed year of 1968 . . . America needs Presidential leadership that can establish a firm focus, and offer a way out of a time of towering uncertainties. Only the President can hold out a vision of the future and rally the people behind it.

The next President must unite America. He must calm its angers, ease its terrible frictions, and bring its people together once again in peace and mutual respect. He has to take *hold* of America before he can move it forward.

This requires leadership that believes in law, and has the courage to enforce it, leadership that believes in justice, and is determined to promote it; leadership that believes in progress, and knows how to inspire it."

turned him down because his liberal views would have made him a difficult running mate. Nixon selected Henry Cabot Lodge instead.

Nixon Versus Kennedy

Nixon's Democratic opponent in the 1960 election was John F. Kennedy, a senator from Massachusetts. The two candidates had numerous similarities. Both had come of age in the 1930s. Both had served in the navy during World War II. Both had Senate experience. Although Nixon was a Republican and Kennedy a Democrat, both took moderate stands on many issues.

The two men also had distinct differences. Kennedy was part of a wealthy family, while Nixon's family was relatively poor. As vice-president, Nixon was better known throughout the country than Kennedy. Nixon also had more experience in foreign policy. Kennedy, on the other hand, was respected in political circles for his brilliant mind and razor-sharp wit. Of the two men, Kennedy was by far more handsome than the jowly Nixon, a difference that would affect the campaign.

The highlight of the 1960 campaign was a series of television debates between Nixon and Kennedy. Nixon had been a debater in high school and college. He had demolished his 1946 congressional candidate in a series of debates. From the Checkers speech, he knew how powerful television could be. Still, Nixon was reluctant to take part in these debates.

> An incumbent seldom agrees willingly to debate his challenger, and I knew the debates would benefit Kennedy more than me by giving his views national exposure which he needed more than I did. Further, he would have the tactical advantage of being on the offensive. As a member of Eisenhower's administration, I would have to defend the administration's record while trying to move the discussion to my own plans and programs. But there was no way I could refuse to debate without having Kennedy and the media turn my refusal into a central campaign issue. The question we faced was not whether to debate, but how to arrange the debates so as to give Kennedy the least possible advantage.[17]

The two candidates agreed to a series of four debates. The first and fourth would follow a debate-style format. The opening debate would cover domestic issues. The final debate would cover foreign policy, which Nixon considered his strongest area. The second and third debates would be, in effect, joint press conferences.

In arranging this format, Nixon made what he later believed was a serious mis-take. He thought the debates would draw larger television audiences as the series progressed. Instead, the audiences became smaller. Fewer Americans heard Nixon's comments on foreign affairs than had heard his initial debate with Kennedy.

Nixon also had bad luck before the debates. He injured his knee, which became infected, and he had to be hospitalized. When he arrived for the first debate, he was underweight and looked drawn and pale. His shirt collar hung loosely about his neck. Nixon made another mistake when he declined makeup.

Kennedy, on the other hand, appeared tanned and handsome on camera. He immediately attacked the Eisenhower administration's record on domestic issues and put Nixon on the defensive. Nixon instantly realized that he had underestimated Kennedy as a debate opponent. He appeared shaken on camera. When the debate was over, Nixon later recalled, many people, including his mother, called to see if he was ill.

During their television debates, Nixon appeared nervous and ill while Kennedy seemed handsome and calm.

Kennedy a Clear Winner

Reporting on the first televised debate between Nixon and John F. Kennedy, the October 10, 1960, issue of Time *magazine observed that Nixon won on points of argument but lost on image.*

"On sound points of argument Nixon probably took most of the honors; a private poll organized by Atlanta *Constitution* publisher Ralph McGill reported Nixon a clear winner to those who listened only by radio. But since the debate shed little new light on the issues of the campaign, some 73 million televiewers were left with the sharp image of the campaigners themselves: two well-informed men, quick with figures and fact, talking quickly against the clock. . . . Kennedy was alert, aggressive and cool. Nixon was strangely nervous, perspiring profusely, so badly made up (by order of his own TV advisor, who decreed a light powdering instead of pancake make-up) that under the baleful glare of floodlights he looked ill as well as ill at ease."

Polls conducted after the debate indicated that many television viewers awarded a victory to Kennedy. The much smaller radio audience, which had not seen the pale and shaken image of Nixon, believed Nixon had won.

Nixon bounced back in the second debate. He wore makeup this time and looked healthy. Both candidates argued their positions on civil rights, economic reform, the political situation in Cuba, and the U. S. position in the cold war. Critics gave the victory to Nixon. *Time* magazine reported that Nixon had landed "an emotional punch" on his Democratic opponent. It was a hollow victory, however, because twenty million fewer viewers watched the debate.

The third and fourth debates, which included the debate on foreign policy issues, provided little new information from either candidate. These debates drew about the same size audience as the second debate.

These debates became the most famous presidential debates in modern history. Many believe that they were the turning point in the campaign, although analysts argue that voters reacted more to the image the candidates projected than to their stand on the issues. Nixon had been ahead of Kennedy in the polls before the debates, but after the debates, polls showed that Kennedy had crept ahead of Nixon. In his memoirs, Nixon discounted such claims, asserting that there were many factors that determine the outcome of an election. He did express

doubt that [debates] can ever serve a responsible role in defining the issues of a presidential campaign. Because of the nature of the medium, there will inevitably be a greater premium on showmanship than on statesmanship.

Nixon's relationship with President Eisenhower also significantly affected his campaign. Nixon had sought out Eisenhower's endorsement very early in his campaign, fearing that Eisenhower might die before he got around to giving it on his own. When asked to campaign for Nixon, Eisenhower promised to set his own campaign schedule, a promise he did not fulfill until the end of the campaign.

In August, Eisenhower made a mistake in a press conference and embarrassed Nixon. When asked to cite major ideas that Vice-President Nixon had contributed to the administration, Eisenhower replied, "If you give me a week, I might think of one." The remark was probably unintentional, but the comment gave the impression that Eisenhower was not very enthusiastic about Nixon's candidacy. Eisenhower later retracted the remark and expressed confidence in his vice-president, but the damage had already been done.

Later in the campaign, Kennedy remarked that the Eisenhower administration had accomplished little and referred to it as eight years of Rip Van Winkle. This criticism finally spurred Eisenhower to campaign on Nixon's behalf. When Eisenhower met with Nixon to arrange his schedule, Nixon said, "Mr. President, I think you've done enough already."

The curt remark stunned aides to both men. Insulted, Eisenhower soon left the meeting. Nixon later explained in his memoirs that Eisenhower did not campaign because both his wife and his doctor had telephoned him to plead that Eisenhower was not well enough to withstand a busy campaign schedule. Eisenhower, however,

Despite his campaign efforts, Nixon lost many black votes when he refused to intervene on behalf of Martin Luther King Jr., who had been arrested in Georgia.

lived for nearly a decade after the 1960 election. It is likely that Nixon no longer wanted Eisenhower's support and was trying to distance himself from the "Rip Van Winkle" administration. Whatever Nixon's motives were, Eisenhower's failure to campaign vigorously for him may have cost Nixon votes.

Another factor that hurt Nixon on election day was his response to the arrest of black civil rights leader Martin Luther King Jr. King had been arrested in a demonstration at a restaurant in Atlanta, Georgia. On a technicality, he was sentenced to four months of hard labor in the Georgia State Penitentiary. King's wife, Coretta, contacted both Nixon and Kennedy for help. Nixon told an aide that King had been given a "bum rap," but he felt it was "completely improper for me or any other lawyer to call the judge." The aide told the press that Nixon had no comment.

Kennedy called Coretta King to express his sympathy. His brother, Robert Kennedy, called the judge and King was soon released on bond. As a result of this incident, much of the black vote swung to Kennedy. Nixon later admitted he had made a mistake.

On Election Day, 68,800,000 votes were cast. Kennedy defeated Nixon by only 113,000 votes. John F. Kennedy was inaugurated on January 20, 1961. That evening, Richard Nixon, now a private citizen for the first time in fourteen years, took a final drive around Washington, D.C. In his memoirs, he recalled thinking that "someday I would be back here."

The Comeback Trail

The Nixon family planned to move back to California. While his daughters finished the school year in Washington, Nixon lived alone in California for six months. He joined the Los Angeles law firm of Adams,

John F. Kennedy was inaugurated in 1961, after defeating Richard Nixon in the presidential campaign.

Duque, and Hazeltine, but neither relocation to California nor practicing law could shake off the disappointment he felt.

> It was not an easy time. . . . I had thought I could move right into the work of the law firm, just as I had done with every other challenging new job. For several weeks, however, I found it difficult to concentrate and almost impossible to work up much enthusiasm. I realized I was experiencing the let down of defeat. . . . I found that virtually everything I did seemed unexciting and unimportant by comparison with national office. . . . The last thing I wanted to do was talk to people about the election.[18]

Despite his disappointment, Nixon never intended to leave politics. While practicing law, he worked on a book called *Six Crises*. The book covered six major events in his political career: The Alger Hiss case, the Fund Crisis, Eisenhower's heart attack, his trip to South America, the debate with Khrushchev, and the 1960 election. As he wrote, Nixon started planning his comeback. He believed that President Kennedy would be unbeatable in 1964. After much consideration, he decided to run for governor of California in 1962. The governorship would keep him involved in politics, while another Republican candidate was sacrificed to Kennedy in 1964.

On September 27, 1961, Nixon announced that he would not be a presidential candidate in 1964, but he would be a candidate for governor in 1962, challenging Governor Edmund Brown. The decision to run had been a difficult one. Nixon knew he was not very interested in being governor and that despite his claims to the contrary, he was using the office as a stepping-stone to the presidency.

Nixon signs copies of his book Six Crises *as part of his campaign for governor of California.*

Nixon's campaign reunited him with Murray Choitner, who had helped organize his victorious "dirty tricks" campaigns in 1946 and 1950. Choitner used his old campaign tactics. Bumper stickers reading "Is Brown pink?" began appearing on cars. Phony campaign literature made up to look like it was distributed by concerned Democrats warned that Brown was influenced by left-wing extremists. But the times had changed, and Nixon's old campaign methods did not work. Communism was no longer a hot campaign issue, and Nixon's efforts to portray Brown as a communist sympathizer failed.

Nixon himself was embroiled in a lingering financial scandal. In 1956 while he was vice-president, he had quietly helped his brother Donald secure a $205,000 loan from billionaire Howard Hughes. Shortly after the loan was made, the Internal Revenue Service (IRS) reversed an earlier ruling and granted tax-exempt status to the Howard Hughes Medical Institute. This change amounted to tens of millions of dollars in savings to the institute. Despite suspicion that Nixon had arranged the reversal of the IRS ruling as a favor to Hughes, the allegation was never proved.

Suspicion about Nixon's role in the scandal lingered in California during 1962. Nixon faced repeated questions about it during news conferences. He was often evasive about the incident. By his own claim, he answered questions relating to the scandal one hundred times.

Nixon's favorable relationship with the California press had also changed. In his earlier campaigns, the *Los Angeles Times* had given its unqualified support to Nixon. Now, the *Times* was under new management and was committed to giving balanced coverage to both Nixon and Brown. The *Times* also exposed some of the Nixon campaign's dirty tricks.

Perhaps most seriously, the public perceived that Nixon's real interests lay not in being governor but in being president of the United States. Nixon himself betrayed his real interest in a speech, when he mistakenly said that he wanted to be "Governor of the United States," a blunder that was reported in the *Los Angeles Times*.

Nixon got up the morning after the election to confirm what he had already sensed. He had lost by 297,000 votes out of 6 million votes cast. In his concession speech, his bitterness erupted in an attack on the press.

All I can say is this: for sixteen years, ever since the Hiss case, you've had a lot of—alot of fun—that you've had the opportunity to attack me and I think I've given as good as I've taken.

I leave you gentlemen now and you will now write it. You will interpret it. That's your right. But as I leave you I want you to know—just think how much you're going to be missing.

You won't have Nixon to kick around anymore, because, gentlemen, this is my last press conference.[19]

Nixon's aides were staggered by this rare public display of anger that they had seen Nixon unleash in private many times throughout his career. Newspaper columnists wrote that Nixon had destroyed his career with the attack. Nixon later wrote in his memoirs that he never regretted this attack on the press. He believed that the attack halted the "biased coverage" and resulted in "much fairer treatment . . . during the next few years."

Sitting One Out

The Nixon family left California in 1963 and moved to New York City, where Nixon joined a Wall Street law firm. The new job allowed Nixon to travel throughout the world and meet with the leaders of many countries. In one trip, he visited Vietnam and observed "how dangerously different the reality of the situation was in Vietnam from the version of it being presented to the American people at home." It seemed to Nixon that the United States spent years developing an anticommunist government in South Vietnam but now seemed unwilling to make the commitment to stop communism.

On November 22, 1963, Nixon heard the horrifying news that President Kennedy had been assassinated in Dallas, Texas. Coincidentally, Nixon had been in Dallas on business only hours before the assassination and first heard the news while traveling by cab from the airport to his New York apartment. He learned months later that he, too, had been a target of Lee Harvey Oswald, Kennedy's accused killer. A few weeks before Kennedy was killed, Oswald had declared to his wife his intentions to kill Nixon, but she had talked him out of it.

Lyndon Johnson, who succeeded Kennedy as president, became the Democratic candidate in 1964. Nixon held to his plan to sit out the 1964 election. In the wake of the assassination, Nixon felt that the country had transferred its loyalty from Kennedy to Johnson. Now, Johnson seemed unbeatable in the election.

Lyndon B. Johnson, Kennedy's successor, seemed unbeatable in the 1964 presidential election.

The Republican party nominated Barry Goldwater, a conservative senator from Arizona. Although Nixon supported Goldwater throughout the campaign, he thought of Goldwater as an inept candidate. Rather than uniting the party, Goldwater alienated its moderate and liberal members with his ultraconservative views on many issues.

Goldwater and Johnson differed widely on the campaign issues, especially on the worsening situation in Vietnam. The French had withdrawn from Vietnam in 1954, and by treaty Vietnam had been temporarily divided into communist North and democratic South Vietnam. The United States had supported South Vietnam's fight against communist guerrillas and North Vietnamese soldiers. To prevent the fall of South Vietnam to communism, the United States had been forced to increase its commitment. Beginning in 1961, President Kennedy had increased the number of U.S. advisory personnel in Vietnam from about nine hundred to nearly sixteen thousand. Kennedy was assassinated before he made the decision either to become further involved in Vietnam or to withdraw altogether.

Goldwater and Johnson took different positions on what the United States should do about South Vietnam. Goldwater favored American military action in South Vietnam to prevent it from falling to the communists. This alarmed many voters. Johnson campaigned as a peace candidate. He did not advocate strong American military action in Vietnam.

On August 2, 1964, North Vietnamese gunboats attacked the American destroyer *Maddox,* which was patrolling off the North Vietnamese coast in the Gulf of Tonkin. A week later, Congress passed the Gulf of Tonkin Resolution, which gave Johnson authorization to protect U.S. advisory forces in Vietnam. Johnson ordered bombing raids against North Vietnam in retaliation for its attacks on American ships off the coast.

Even though his actions seemed to contradict his position as a peace candidate, Johnson won the election in a landslide. In addition, the Republicans lost seats in the House and Senate and in many state legislatures around the country.

Early in 1965, Nixon evaluated his position. The Republican party, he believed, was breaking apart and he saw himself as the man who could unify it. His plan was to work toward unifying the Republican party for the 1966 congressional elections. If he was successful, the party would regain

Lyndon Johnson committed increasing numbers of troops to the war in Vietnam in hopes of keeping the country out of communist hands.

President Johnson watches the polls as he is reelected in a landslide victory.

its lost ground, and he would have a stronger base from which to launch his own campaign for the presidency in 1968. Nixon said:

> I had finally come to the realization that there was no other life for me but politics and public service. Even when my legal work was at its most interesting I never found it truly fulfilling. I told some friends at this time that if all I had was my legal work, I would be mentally dead in two years and physically dead in four. I knew that they thought I was exaggerating; but I was telling the truth about the way I thought and felt.[20]

The 1968 Election

Throughout the next three years, Nixon quietly worked toward his goal to become president. He continued his world travels. He spoke out on domestic and foreign policy issues, keeping his name in the national spotlight. Throughout 1966, Nixon campaigned for Republican candidates around the country. It is hard to measure Nixon's contribution, but the Republicans recaptured many of the seats they lost two years earlier.

Immediately after the 1966 elections, Nixon announced he was taking a six-month holiday from politics. Privately, however, he met with old friends and advisers and ordered them to proceed with plans to secure his nomination for president in 1968.

On February 2, 1968, Nixon officially announced his candidacy in a speech he gave in New Hampshire. In a rare display of humor, Nixon began his speech by referring to his bitter press conference after his defeat in the 1962 election. "Gentlemen," he said, "this is *not* my last press conference."

The country that Nixon planned to lead had changed dramatically since 1964. The public was divided by the Vietnam War. Minority groups were marching to demand their civil rights. Rock and roll, experimental drug use, and the sexual revolution had widened the generation gap between parents and children.

Nixon presented himself to Americans as a presidential candidate who could bring

A Bitterly Fought Election

Newsweek magazine explained why the 1968 presidential election was so close in its November 11 issue of that year.

"Part of the answer was clearly the third-party candidacy of George Wallace . . . the ultimate effect of the Wallace campaign was to deny a really decisive victory to Nixon by depriving him of any Deep South reserve.

Another part of the answer lay in the kind of campaigns waged by Nixon and Humphrey. For his part, Nixon built his base on a block of electoral votes from the Border and Western states and directed his 'law and order' appeal at the silent voters of middle America. . . . There were also the factors of Nixon's own standoffish, above-the-issues campaign, his refusal to debate Humphrey and his choice of Spiro T. Agnew as his running mate. None of the major issues—Vietnam, law and order or race—seemed to produce any massive move to Nixon. . . . Richard Nixon . . . knew perhaps better than anyone else that what he had won was a bitterly fought election, not a mandate. The issues that divided the nation were still there."

President Nixon and Spiro Agnew are congratulated by supporters.

new leadership to the country. He easily worked his way through the presidential primaries. Despite an eleventh-hour challenge by Ronald Reagan, Nixon won the Republican party's nomination on the first ballot in August 1968. He selected Maryland governor Spiro T. Agnew as his running mate.

Nixon's Democratic opponent was Vice-President Hubert H. Humphrey. Humphrey had been nominated after an extraordinary series of events that nearly shattered the Democratic party. In March, President Johnson, damaged by his failure to end the Vietnam War, shocked the nation when he announced that he would not run for reelection. In June, Senator Robert Kennedy, a front-runner for the Democratic nomination, was killed by an assassin shortly after declaring victory in California's presidential primary.

Richard Nixon is sworn in as president of the United States.

Although the race was primarily between Nixon and Humphrey, Nixon also faced another challenger. Alabama governor George Wallace ran for the presidency as a member of the American Independent party. Wallace had little chance of victory, but he could influence which major party candidate won.

The main campaign issue was Vietnam. Nixon promised to resolve the Vietnam War. Humphrey also promised to end the war but had difficulty in disassociating himself from Johnson's failed Vietnam policies. He began to gain ground in the later stages of the campaign, boosted by President Johnson's halting of the bombing runs against North Vietnam.

Americans went to the polls on November 5. The race between Nixon and Humphrey was so close that few were willing to risk a prediction. The suspense lasted until almost noon the next day. The voters had elected Richard M. Nixon to be the thirty-seventh president of the United States in the closest presidential election in history.

The civil rights movement challenged the government to provide effective legislation and leadership.

6 Foreign Policy

In his inaugural speech on January 20, 1969, Nixon told Americans, "I shall consecrate my office, energies and all the wisdom I can summon, to the cause of peace among nations." Ending the war in Vietnam was Nixon's top priority. Since President Johnson first sent American combat troops to Vietnam in 1965, the war had evolved into a stalemate, with neither the communists nor the American-supported South Vietnamese able to secure a final victory. In January 1968, the communists supported by North Vietnam launched the Tet Offensive, an all-out invasion of South Vietnam. By the end of April, American and South Vietnamese soldiers had beaten the communists back, but many Americans concluded that victory in Vietnam was unachievable.

Nixon sought what he would later call an honorable peace in Vietnam. He wanted not only to bring peace but at the same time to reassure other countries throughout the world that the United States would not abandon its commitments to them.

Nixon wanted to reduce America's active role in Vietnam by returning the responsibility for fighting the communists to the South Vietnamese, a process he called Vietnamization. Soon after Nixon took office, efforts began to train and equip South Vietnamese soldiers to take the place of American soldiers. In June 1969, Nixon ordered the withdrawal of twenty-five thousand American troops. Troop withdrawals continued while Nixon implemented his other policies. Vietnamization, Nixon hoped, would lessen antiwar protests at home and give him time to pursue the kind of peace he wanted.

The Tet Offensive, launched in 1968, almost destroyed Saigon.

Nixon explains the plan for expanding military operations into Cambodia and Laos.

Expanding the War

Nixon also expanded the fighting into the neighboring countries of Cambodia and Laos. This policy was in direct opposition to Johnson's war strategy. Johnson had feared that expanding the war into neighboring countries might draw China or the Soviet Union into the fighting. Nixon believed this would not happen. He understood that if he did not expand the war, the North Vietnamese could continue to resupply themselves from the Ho Chi Minh Trail that wound through Laos and Cambodia or seek sanctuary in those countries.

Soon after his inauguration, Nixon ordered secret bombing raids inside Cambodia, where communist troops sought sanctuary and stored war supplies. In April 1970, Nixon took even stronger action by authorizing a ground invasion of Cambodia by South Vietnamese troops, assisted by American forces. On April 31, he appeared on national television to announce his plans and explain his motives.

The action I have taken tonight is indispensable for the continuing success of [our troop] withdrawal program. A majority of the American people want to end this war rather than to have it drag on interminably. The action I have taken tonight will serve that purpose. . . . We take this action not for the purpose of expanding the war into Cambodia but for the purpose of ending the war in Vietnam, and winning the just peace we all desire. We have made and will continue to make every possible effort to end this war through negotiation at the conference table rather than through more fighting in the battlefield.[21]

The invasion caught the communists by surprise. They abandoned their headquarters and left behind tons of supplies.

Despite the invasion's success, the U.S. Senate felt that Nixon had overstepped his constitutional powers by expanding the war into Cambodia. The Constitution explicitly states that Congress, not the president, has the right to declare war. On June 24, the Senate voted to repeal the Gulf of Tonkin Resolution to protest the invasion. Six days later, the Senate passed an amendment that barred further military action in Cambodia.

Many Americans, too, disagreed with the action. They believed it was immoral because American security was not at risk. They also saw Nixon's action as an expansion of a war he had promised to end. Protests erupted across the country in reaction to the invasion, especially on college campuses. Nixon, in turn, was angered by the protests. He called the protestors "bums" and appealed to the "silent majority" of Americans for support of his action.

The protests on college campuses quickly escalated. The National Guard was sent to twenty-one colleges and universities to help restore order. On Monday, May 4, National Guard troops suddenly fired upon demonstrating students at Kent State University in Ohio. Four students were shot dead, and nine were wounded. To discourage further protests, some universities suspended classes for the remainder of the school year. The intensity of the protests cooled as campuses shut down and the school year ended. Although Nixon's actions remained unpopular among many college students and faculty members, the violence stopped.

Despite the Senate vote and the unpopularity of his actions, Nixon continued with his strategy. In February 1971, South Vietnamese troops invaded Laos in a ground military operation known as the Lam Son 719 Campaign. This time, the communists had advance warning and routed the South Vietnamese soldiers. American planes launched a massive bombing attack against the communists, which prevented

(left) Protests against the American military presence in Vietnam were staged at many college campuses.

(right) At Kent State University in Ohio, National Guard troops killed four students who were participating in an antiwar demonstration.

Nixon kept his promise to remove American troops from South Vietnam.

the Lam Son 719 Campaign from being a complete military disaster.

The ultimate failure of the operation caused many military and political figures in the United States to reconsider Nixon's Vietnamization strategy. The near defeat of the South Vietnamese made them wonder if Vietnamization, now in its second year, was working and if the South Vietnamese would ever be able to defend themselves against the communists.

While the success of his Vietnamization and expansion strategies were debated, Nixon kept his promise to bring American troops home. By mid-1971, nearly half of the more than 500,000 American troops had been withdrawn.

China and the Soviet Union

Like his predecessors, Nixon viewed the war in Vietnam as a battle against the further expansion of communism. But unlike his predecessors, Nixon actively sought to engage America's communist "enemies" in finding a solution to the Vietnam War. In 1972, Nixon initiated new diplomatic policies that improved American relations with the Soviet Union and China and also gave him leverage to use against North Vietnam in his efforts to end the fighting.

Nixon first attempted to secure diplomatic ties with China. Communists had taken control of China in 1949. The United States had refused to recognize this new communist government as the rightful government. Diplomatic ties and all trade with China had been suspended. Nixon thought that this policy was foolish. Late in 1971, Nixon relaxed U.S. trade restrictions against China. In February 1972, he stunned the world by visiting China himself and meeting with its communist leaders.

This historic trip "opened" China to the United States once again. It served as a starting point for reestablishing diplomatic and trade relations between the two countries. Opening China is considered one of Nixon's most important diplomatic accomplishments.

The End of Anticommunism

The March 6, 1972, issue of Time *magazine offered a perspective on the significance of President Nixon's historic visit to China in February 1972.*

"In the long run, one of the most important questions about the U.S. and China will be just how much the two countries may learn from each other. For the nearer future, though, the President's trip must be judged in terms of world politics. In the U.S., it almost certainly formalized the end of anti-Communism as a dominant foreign policy—and it was fitting that Richard Nixon should help end that era as dramatically as he once helped start it.

The trip also marked the beginning of a more pragmatic and complex, less concentrated and crusading application of American power."

Nixon and his wife Pat visit the Great Wall of China during their tour of China.

At the same time that he was establishing this new relationship with China, Nixon was also taking steps to decrease the tension between the United States and the Soviet Union. The two great nations had struggled for nearly thirty years to counteract the other's influence around the globe. The two countries had become locked in a nuclear arms race that neither could halt without being vulnerable to attack. Although Nixon had begun his political career as a dedicated anticommunist, he recognized that the time was right for a more pragmatic approach to the problems the two nations faced.

The Nixon administration first entered Strategic Arms Limitation Talks (SALT)

Nixon and Brezhnev sign the SALT I agreement in May 1972.

1972, Nixon became the first American president to visit the Soviet capital when he journeyed to Moscow to participate in a summit conference with Soviet leaders. The climax of the summit came when the two countries signed a historic agreement known as SALT I that placed limitations on antiballistic missiles.

Nixon's new policy toward the Soviet Union was called detente, a French word meaning "the easing of strained relations." The SALT agreement reduced tensions between the two superpowers, and a new phase in their relationship developed. An atmosphere of mutual understanding and cooperation replaced the inflexible positions they had maintained toward each other since the end of World War II. For Nixon, detente and the SALT agreement were a diplomatic triumph, capping years of effort. Even Nixon's toughest critics agree that detente ranks as an outstanding achievement in foreign policy.

with the Soviets in 1969. In 1972, Nixon sensed that the time was right for final negotiations with the Soviet Union. In May

Keeping the Balance of Terror

The June 5, 1972, issue of Time *magazine found that the arms agreements completed at the 1972 U.S.-Soviet summit made "sound sense."*

"In broad perspective, the agreements formalized the U.S. shift from the Eisenhower-Kennedy insistence upon 'nuclear superiority' to what the Nixon Administration terms 'nuclear sufficiency.' Since the Soviet Union was intent upon reaching at least parity with the U.S. and since both sides possess a tremendous overkill capability, the new U.S. stance makes sound sense. In agreeing that defensive missiles will be limited to two sites in each nation and that no more offensive ballistic missiles will be installed, the U.S. risks little; the 'balance of terror' will not be upset to the advantage of either side."

The Road to Peace in Vietnam

Nixon hoped that the opening of China and detente with the Soviet Union would do more than improve America's relationship with those countries. He wanted China and the Soviet Union to put pressure on North Vietnam to end the fighting in South Vietnam. Nixon did this by linking the interests of China and the Soviet Union to a solution in Vietnam that was acceptable to the United States. In effect, Nixon told leaders of both China and the Soviet Union that until the Vietnam War was ended, he could not approve grain exports to their nations. Nixon's critics remain divided over whether this strategy made any significant contribution to ending the Vietnam War.

Henry Kissinger and Le Duc Tho meet in an attempt to secure peace in Vietnam.

Secret Negotiations

Formal peace negotiations between the United States and North Vietnam had opened in Paris in 1969. Early in 1970, Nixon became convinced that the delicate issues that had to be negotiated to reach a peace settlement could not be discussed publicly. He sent his national security adviser, Henry Kissinger, to negotiate secretly with North Vietnamese negotiator Le Duc Tho. The two diplomats met secretly for two years without a breakthrough in their negotiations.

Hopes for peace were nearly dashed in the spring of 1972 when North Vietnam launched a large offensive against the South. The North Vietnamese hoped that a successful offensive would give them control of South Vietnamese territory. The communists also knew that Nixon faced reelection in November. They hoped that he would be willing to make concessions to end the fighting quickly so that his chances for reelection would be better.

The communists soon occupied many towns throughout South Vietnam. With U.S. air assistance, the South Vietnamese army fought back. Throughout the summer, the South Vietnamese recaptured the towns that the communists had occupied at the beginning of the offensive. By September, most of the territory had been reclaimed. Even though the South Vietnamese ultimately prevailed on the battlefield, the North Vietnamese maintained the strategic advantage. To many Americans, the heavy losses that the South Vietnamese had suffered at the beginning of the Spring Offensive proved that South Vietnam was incapable of defeating the communists without continued assistance from the United States.

As the offensive continued, the stalled peace negotiations suddenly became active again, as both sides recognized the need to begin serious negotiations. As the communists had foreseen, Nixon was running for reelection in November. He had been elected in 1968 by promising to achieve peace in Vietnam. In 1972, the war was again a major campaign issue. Nixon's Democratic opponent, George McGovern, promised an immediate end to "Nixon's war" if elected, which put pressure on Nixon to make progress in securing his vision of peace before the election. Nixon's other policies—Vietnamization, expanding the war, and pursuing detente—had not produced the peace Nixon had promised. Negotiating suddenly looked like the best way to achieve peace.

George McGovern campaigns against Nixon for the presidency.

The North Vietnamese were also more willing to enter serious negotiations because their army had suffered heavy losses during the Spring Offensive. Peace negotiations would give the North Vietnamese a break in the fighting and time to rebuild and resupply their depleted armies. The North Vietnamese also believed that Nixon might be more willing to make concessions in order to reach a settlement before the election.

Negotiations began in July between Henry Kissinger and Le Duc Tho. A settlement was nearly completed in early October. The settlement called for a cease-fire in all of Southeast Asia. The United States would withdraw its remaining troops in sixty days. South Vietnamese president Nguyen Van Thieu would be allowed to remain in power. U.S. prisoners of war would be returned. The various Vietnamese political parties would be left alone to decide the future of South Vietnam. The United States agreed to allow some North Vietnamese troops to remain in South Vietnam.

Before a final settlement was reached, however, a complicated series of events derailed the peace talks. President Thieu of South Vietnam rejected the agreement outright because he feared it left him too vulnerable. Without U.S. support, he knew he could not survive in office. Nixon did not want to abandon Thieu and instructed Kissinger to negotiate further.

Nixon's critics charged that Nixon himself developed second thoughts about the agreement and that he used Thieu's objections as an excuse to continue negotiations. The agreement, his critics say, contained all of the terms important to the United States, but opinion polls in the United States indicated that Nixon would win reelection in

November whether or not the treaty was signed. With his reelection certain, Nixon delayed signing the treaty in an effort to get additional concessions from the North Vietnamese, his critics claim.

The North Vietnamese concluded that U.S. procrastination in signing the treaty was a signal that the Americans were trying to back out of the agreement. In an effort to force the United States to accept the tentative agreement, Le Duc Tho went public on October 24 with the secret talks and the terms that had so far been negotiated. Le Duc Tho's maneuver made it appear to the rest of the world that the United States was responsible for the snag in the negotiations. To counteract Le Duc Tho's move, Kissinger declared on October 26 that "peace is at hand." From this point, the negotiations deteriorated rapidly. Final negotiations were delayed until after the presidential election.

A quick end to the Vietnam War was not the decisive issue in the 1972 presidential election. Nixon's opponent, George McGovern, had promised to end the war immediately if elected. Many Americans believed that McGovern had no plans beyond ending the war, however. Despite the fact that Nixon had not been able to end that war during his first term, his other achievements and his plans for the future more than made up for it. Nixon won the election in a landslide, receiving more popular votes than any presidential candidate in history.

When the talks resumed after the election, both sides made demands that the other rejected. The talks broke off on December 13. Nixon's peace efforts were now threatened by both South Vietnam and North Vietnam. To convince Thieu to accept the settlement, Nixon promised future aid and assistance and threatened to sign a treaty without him. Thieu reluctantly agreed, knowing he had no alternative.

Nixon now had to convince the North Vietnamese to agree to a settlement they had already agreed to in early October. Nixon recalled in his memoirs:

Nixon and Spiro Agnew celebrate their reelection.

The Christmas Bombings

Nixon's memoirs explain why he ordered the Christmas bombings in North Vietnam in 1972, one of the most controversial acts he took in his efforts to end the war.

"I had reluctantly decided that we had now reached the point where only the strongest action would have any effect in convincing Hanoi that negotiating a fair settlement with us was a better option for them than continuing the war. Kissinger and I agreed that this meant stepping up the bombing. The only question was how much bombing would be needed to force Hanoi to settle. Kissinger recommended reseeding the mines of Haiphong Harbor, resuming full-scale bombing south of the 20th parallel, and intensifying bombing in south Laos. My intuition was that something far more extensive was required. When I checked and found that the area south of the 20th parallel was largely rice paddies and jungle, I told Kissinger, 'We'll take the same heat for big blows as for little blows. If we renew the bombing, it will have to be something new, and that means we will have to make the big decision to hit Hanoi and Haiphong with B-52s. Anything less will only make the enemy contemptuous.'... The order to renew bombing the week before Christmas was the most difficult decision I made during the entire war; at the same time, however, it was also one of the most clear-cut and necessary ones."

I had reluctantly decided that we had now reached the point where only the strongest action would have any effect in convincing Hanoi that negotiating a fair settlement with us was a better option for them than continuing the war. Kissinger and I agreed that this meant stepping up the bombing. The only question was how much bombing would be needed to force Hanoi to settle.[22]

Beginning on December 18, American B-52 bombers pounded the North Vietnamese cities of Hanoi and Haiphong for twelve straight days, except for Christmas Day. The air attacks were some of the heaviest bombing raids of the entire war.

The Christmas bombings outraged Americans. Once again, Nixon seemed to be expanding the war when peace was at hand. On December 30, the Democrats in the House and Senate voted overwhelmingly to cut off funds for continuing the war in Vietnam. Nixon was warned that Congress would move to end the war if he could not. The North Vietnamese agreed on December 28 to resume talks on January 2. Critics still debate whether the brutal Christmas bombings influenced their decision.

An agreement very similar to the one reached in early October was quickly formalized. On January 24, 1973, four days after Nixon had been inaugurated for his second term as president, he went on national television to announce a peace settlement.

The cease-fire went into effect on January 27, 1973. After four years of effort, President Nixon had finally achieved an honorable peace in Vietnam. An editorial in the *New York Times* expressed the feelings of many Americans.

The Vietnam agreement announced by President Nixon last night after more than four years of false starts and disappointed hopes could mark a momentous turning point for the United States, for Southeast Asia and for the world. For the United States, the agreement signals the end of a nightmare,

An Immoral Strategy

On December 10, 1972, the New York Times *published a stinging editorial denouncing President Nixon's use of bombers to bring North Vietnam back to the negotiating table.*

"President Nixon has resorted once more to naked force to try to obtain his own larger objectives in Southeast Asia—objectives which are neither realistic nor essential to this country's security interests. However much Hanoi may be responsible for disrupting the negotiations—which is a highly disputed point—civilized man will be horrified at the renewed spectacle of the world's mightiest air force mercilessly pounding a small Asian nation in an abuse of national power and disregard of humanitarian principles. . . . Although the bombs unquestionably are aimed at military targets, there can be no doubt that they will inflict terrible suffering on civilians in the heavily populated Hanoi-Haiphong area and other population centers. By thus raising the cost of continuing resistance, the President evidently hopes to induce North Vietnam's leaders to abandon their struggle of nearly three decades and agree to his terms. Even if this were morally acceptable strategy, all experience argues against its success . . . the United States . . . is in danger of being reduced to a kind of Stone Age barbarism that could destroy some of what is most worth preserving in American civilization."

Henry Kissinger and Le Duc Tho sign a cease-fire settlement.

the lifting of a staggering burden from the nation's resources, energies and conscience. It promises the speedy and safe return of American troops and prisoners and an opportunity for fresh beginnings on neglected problems at home and abroad.[23]

Nixon's critics charged that the settlement was not a real peace but a negotiated withdrawal of American troops. Others declared that a similar settlement could have been negotiated four years earlier. During those four years of unnecessary fighting, thousands more American soldiers had died in Vietnam.

But most Americans were delighted that the "nightmare" of Vietnam was finally over. Public opinion polls showed that Nixon had never been more popular during his presidency.

Nixon and the Supreme Court

In addition to his foreign policy achievements, Nixon also influenced domestic policy during his first term. Foremost was his appointment of four new justices to the Supreme Court, the nation's highest court. Warren Earl Burger was sworn in as the nation's new chief justice on June 23, 1969. Harry A. Blackmun took his seat in June 1970, followed by Lewis F. Powell and William H. Rehnquist, who were confirmed in December 1971.

Not since President Warren Harding appointed four judges in the 1920s had a single president had such an opportunity to influence the tone and direction of the Supreme Court. Nixon's appointments were

Nixon appointed four conservative Supreme Court justices: Warren Earl Burger (front row, center), Lewis F. Powell (back row, first on left), Harry A. Blackmun (back row, third from left), and William H. Rehnquist (back row, fourth from left).

intended to reverse the liberal direction the Court had taken during the previous twenty years. The appointments did change its tone, but the "Nixon Court" surprised critics with numerous liberal decisions, including one of the most controversial decisions in modern history. In January 1973, in the case of *Roe v. Wade*, the Court voted seven to two to legalize abortion. The Court also struck down the death penalty and redefined obscenity in the early 1970s. The Court later reversed its death penalty ruling.

Nixon's four appointees served together on the bench for fourteen years. In 1992, Blackmun and Rehnquist were still on the Court. Nixon's indirect influence on American law will be felt until they leave the bench.

President Nixon himself would have little time to savor these achievements. Almost immediately after the announcement of peace in Vietnam, a new nightmare enveloped America. The Watergate scandal would do what the Alger Hiss case, the Fund Crisis, the lost election of 1960, and Vietnam had not done. It would bring about the downfall of Richard Nixon.

7 Watergate: The Fall

With Vietnam finally behind him, President Nixon began his second term with high hopes. He intended to lead a "new American revolution" by restructuring and streamlining the bulky federal government. He hoped to build on the foreign policy achievements of his first term. Instead, Nixon's involvement in the Watergate scandal would overshadow most of his plans for his second term and ultimately destroy his presidency.

The scandal that slowly consumed Nixon during his second term actually began near the end of his first term, when he was just beginning to campaign for reelection. In the early morning hours of June 17, 1972, five burglars with electronic listening equipment, or bugs, and large amounts of cash were arrested inside the Democratic party's national headquarters in the posh Watergate office and residence complex in Washington, D.C.

Numerous organizations, including the FBI and the Central Intelligence Agency (CIA), quickly entered the case. The media also began its own investigation. During the next two years, the various investigators would both cooperate with each other and compete as they tried to piece the complicated Watergate story together.

In June 1972, burglars with electronic listening equipment were arrested inside the Democratic party headquarters in the Watergate complex.

An immediate link between the burglary and the Nixon administration was discovered. One of the burglars arrested, James W. McCord Jr., worked as a security consultant for the Committee to Reelect the President (CRP), the organization formed to run President Nixon's 1972 reelection campaign.

On June 18, President Nixon routinely assigned the handling of the Watergate problem to John Ehrlichman, his chief domestic affairs adviser. On the day after the break-in, Nixon believed that the incident was an embarrassing but relatively unimportant issue that could be smoothed over with a proper public relations effort. Ehrlichman's job was to coordinate that public relations effort.

But the break-in was far more serious. It was a crime. The arrest of the five burglars generated a host of questions. What were the burglars doing inside the Democratic party's headquarters? Who had hired

John Ehrlichman was a central figure in the Watergate cover-up.

them? What connection did the burglars have to the White House and to President Nixon? Did Nixon know about the break-in in advance? Had Nixon planned the break-in himself?

The Nixon administration's efforts to cover up the answers to these and other related questions became the central issue of Watergate. In the days immediately following the break-in, few details reached the public. On June 22, President Nixon made his first public statement about the Watergate burglary in a press conference. He denied any White House involvement and declared that "attempted surveillance" had no place in the governmental process.

In truth, Nixon had not had advance knowledge of the break-in and easily could have said so. But he feared the political damage of being linked to the break-in in any way. So, rather than suffer whatever political embarrassment the truth might have caused him, Nixon instead ordered the incident to be covered up, setting the tone for the handling of Watergate by his aides. Had he told the truth in this press conference, the tragic, historic events that unfolded over the next two years might never have occurred.

On June 23, Nixon met with his chief of staff, H. R. Haldeman. Haldeman briefed him on the Watergate problem.

> Now, on the investigation, you know the Democratic break-in thing, we're back in the problem area because the F.B.I. is not under control, because [acting F.B.I. director Patrick] Gray doesn't exactly know how to control it and they have—their investigation is now leading into some productive areas—because they've been able to

Nixon walks with H. R. Haldeman, whom he directed to "control" the FBI by declaring the Watergate incident a national security affair.

Widening Investigations

Details about Watergate developed over the next six months as official investigators and reporters from the media sought answers to the many Watergate questions. Each answer, however, seemed to generate new questions. Clues about the burglary and the subsequent cover-up seemed to lead beyond the Committee to Reelect the President straight into the White House. As the investigations uncovered more and more illegal activities unrelated to the break-in, the term *Watergate* began to refer to an astonishing and ever-widening record of corruption within the Nixon administration.

The investigators found evidence that the administration had accepted illegal campaign contributions, had supported other illegal break-ins, and had granted favors to big business in return for campaign contributions. They also discovered evidence of "dirty tricks" against Democratic candidates that ranged from ordering large quantities of pizza to be delivered to nonexistent Democratic rallies to the writing of a letter that severely damaged the presidential campaign of Senator Edmund Muskie. Just before the New Hampshire presidential primary, a fake letter planted in the media made Muskie appear to be prejudiced against the many New Hampshire voters of French-Canadian descent. Publication of this letter marked the beginning of Muskie's decline as a candidate. Authorship of the letter was later traced to Ken Clausen, a White House staff member.

The investigations discovered that many of these illegal activities were carried out by a team of men calling themselves the Plumbers. The Plumbers operated out

trace the money [the burglars possessed when arrested]—not through the money itself—but through the bank sources—the banker. And, and it goes in some directions we don't want it to go.[24]

Nixon and Haldeman decided to "control" the FBI by having the CIA tell the bureau to stay out of the investigation because it was a matter of national security. "Play it tough," Nixon told Haldeman that day. "That's the way they play it and that's the way we are going to play it." Nixon's efforts to use the CIA to block the FBI investigation was an abuse of his presidential powers. Although the plan did not succeed, this conversation would come back to haunt Nixon nearly two years later.

of the White House and leaked embarrassing information to the media about other candidates. Frequent targets of the Plumbers were members of the secret White House enemies list. The list contained the names of politicians, members of the press, and others who were considered hostile to or enemies of the Nixon administration.

Many of the dirty tricks and Plumbers' activities were financed through a secret fund maintained and administered by White House staff. As in 1952, a secret fund once again linked Nixon to scandal. The White House fund proved to be more serious than the other, however, because it financed illegal activity.

John Dean advised Nixon on the legal and political aspects of the Watergate scandal.

A Cancer on the Presidency

On March 21, 1973, John Dean, who was President Nixon's legal counsel, met with Nixon. Dean had requested the meeting to "paint a complete picture" of Watergate for the president. Dean quickly summarized the dangerous situation the administration faced. He concluded, "We have a cancer within, close to the Presidency, that is growing. It is growing daily. It's compounded, growing geometrically now, because it compounds itself."

Dean presented many details about the administration's cover-up, most of which Nixon already knew because of his own involvement. To protect himself, Nixon pretended that he was hearing the news for the first time. During the discussion, Dean suggested two possible courses of action, one that would minimize the damage already done and one that would aggressively continue the cover-up.

There are two routes. One is to figure out how to cut the losses and minimize the human impact and get you up and out and away from it in any way. In a way it would never come back to haunt you. That is one general alternative. The other is to go down the road, just hunker down, fight it at every corner, every turn, don't let people testify— cover it up is what we really are talking about. Just keep it buried, and just hope that we can do it, hope that we make good decisions at the right time, keep our heads cool, we make the right moves.[25]

The two men, later joined by Haldeman, discussed Watergate for nearly two hours and met again later that day. They discussed the payment of hush money to continue the silence of the original burglars. They discussed various ways to prevent the Watergate scandal from doing further damage. They considered who might end up going to jail for their roles in the cover-up and other crimes. At the end of the long day, the three men remained undecided about what to do. Ultimately, they continued the cover-up, as Dean had suggested during the day.

But no actions the president and his men could take could halt the Watergate steamroller. Every day, more news about Watergate appeared in the media. The president's closest aides were now implicated in Watergate crimes. It took a scorecard to keep track of what members of the administration were under investigation by which agency.

The investigations implicated Nixon himself. Nixon knew that he had to disassociate himself from the scandal before it reached him. On April 30, 1973, Nixon went on national radio and television to talk about Watergate and announce changes in his administration. He repeated his earlier denials about Watergate, then acknowledged that on March 21, "new information" came to him. Without putting any blame on them, Nixon announced that he was accepting the resignations of his top aides, H. R. Haldeman, John Ehrlichman, and his counsel John Dean, all of whom were now implicated in the cover-up.

In mid-May, two significant events occurred that would set the president on a collision course with disaster. On May 17, 1973, the Senate began televised hearings to investigate Watergate and related issues. On the next day, Archibald Cox, a Harvard University law professor, was appointed special prosecutor by President Nixon himself. Cox's job was to sort out the Watergate Scandal and prosecute those who had committed crimes related to the burglary, the cover-up, and other illegal actions.

(right)
Nixon chose Archibald Cox, being sworn in here, as special prosecutor for the Watergate case.

(left)
John Dean testifies to the Senate about the Watergate scandal after Nixon removed him from his advisory position.

The Senate hearings did not take long to produce more problems for the president. On June 25, John Dean testified before the Senate committee. In his testimony, Dean shocked the nation by directly implicating President Nixon in the Watergate cover-up. Across the country, Americans watched television in fascination and disbelief as the soft-spoken Dean told them that their president had been lying about Watergate for a year. He claimed that Nixon had at least some knowledge of the cover-up from the time of the break-in and had let the cover-up continue through April of 1973, despite being warned of the political and legal dangers. Like the Hiss case and the Fund Crisis, Watergate became a national obsession.

The Watergate Tapes

Despite the sensational nature of Dean's testimony, there was little evidence. It was Dean's word against the word of the president of the United States. Another Nixon aide named Alexander Butterfield, however, made a startling disclosure during testimony on July 16. Butterfield revealed the existence of an elaborate tape-recording system that Nixon had installed in 1970 in the Oval Office and other offices he routinely used.

The discovery of the taping system was a turning point in the Watergate scandal. It meant that a record of Nixon's conversations with his aides existed. These tapes could be used to determine the truth about Watergate. The battle for the tapes quickly became the focus of the Watergate investigations.

Special Prosecutor Archibald Cox and the Senate committee chairman, Sam Ervin, both issued the first of many demands, or subpoenas, for the tapes on July 23. Nixon refused to relinquish the subpoenaed tapes. He knew that there was dangerous evidence on the tapes that would prove that he had been lying about his involvement in the Watergate cover-up from the beginning. To destroy the tapes, now that their existence had been made public, would certainly make him look guilty. Nixon also knew there were conversations on the tapes that he could interpret to reinforce his claims of innocence. As long as he could retain control of them and reveal only selective conversations, Nixon believed the tapes would be an asset to him.

To retain control of the tapes, Nixon said it was his executive privilege to withhold them. Other presidents had used the concept of executive privilege successfully to withhold sensitive information from Congress or the courts.

More Scandal

By midsummer, the Senate Watergate hearings, the battle for the tapes, and the continuous coverage of Watergate by the media had severely damaged Nixon's popularity. A Gallup poll released on August 15 showed that Nixon's approval rating had plummeted from 68 percent in January (after the Vietnam peace agreement) to only 31 percent. The figure was the lowest public approval rating for a president in twenty years.

For Nixon, it seemed that things could hardly get worse, but they did. His personal

Guarding the Privacy of the Presidency

Addressing the nation on April 29, 1974, President Nixon explained why he had refused to relinquish the White House tapes. The address was published in that day's issue of the New York Times.

"Ever since the existence of the White House taping system was first made known last summer, I have tried vigorously to guard the privacy of the tapes. I've been well aware that my effort to protect the confidentiality of Presidential conversations has heightened the sense of mystery about Watergate and, in fact, has caused increased suspicion of the President.

Many people assumed that the tapes must incriminate the President, or that otherwise he wouldn't insist on their privacy. But the problem I confronted was this: Unless a President can protect the privacy of the advice he gets, he cannot get the advice he needs.

This principle is recognized in the constitutional doctrine of executive privilege, which has been defended and maintained by every President since Washington and which has been recognized by the courts whenever tested as inherent in the Presidency.

I consider it to be my constitutional responsibility to defend this principle."

finances also came under investigation. Americans soon learned that Nixon had engaged in questionable real estate deals and had cheated on his income taxes. They were furious.

A scandal unrelated to Watergate further tarnished Nixon's administration. Vice-President Spiro Agnew had been under investigation for corruption during his days as governor of Maryland. On October 10, Agnew finally resigned as vice-president of the United States, after pleading no contest to one count of income tax evasion. Congressman Gerald Ford later replaced him as vice-president.

The United States was now wallowing in Watergate and its related scandals. Both the media and the politicians all but ignored other domestic issues and international affairs. President Nixon himself was unable to concentrate on anything else. His days and nights were filled with meetings about Watergate. He spent hours listening to the tapes. He held meetings with aides to draft responses to endless media reports about the latest allegations. He worked with his lawyers to plan ways to thwart the prosecutor's efforts to secure the tapes.

LATE CITY EDITION

The New York Times

"All the News That's Fit to Print"

VOL.CXXIII...No.42,264   NEW YORK, THURSDAY, OCTOBER 11, 1973   15 CENTS

AGNEW QUITS VICE PRESIDENCY AND ADMITS TAX EVASION IN '67; NIXON CONSULTS ON SUCCESSOR

U.S. Believes Moscow Is Resupplying Arabs by Airlift

Soviet Could Spur Move to Aid Israel

CONGRESS TO VOTE — Opposition Is Hinted if Choice Is Possible 1976 Candidate

Judge Orders Fine, 3 Years' Probation

Agnew Plea Ends 65 Days Of Insisting on Innocence

EVIDENCE SHOWS GIFTS TO AGNEW

Spiro Agnew resigned as vice-president after accusations surfaced of corruption during his term as governor of Maryland.

The Saturday Night Massacre

In October, Nixon offered typed summaries of specific tapes to comply with a subpoena issued by Cox. Cox rejected the summaries and demanded the actual tapes. Nixon decided Cox had to be fired to halt his pursuit of the tapes. On Saturday, October 20, he delegated the job to Attorney General Elliot Richardson. Richardson resigned rather than fire Cox. The job was passed on to Deputy Attorney General William Ruckelshaus, who also refused. Rather than accept his resignation, Nixon fired Ruckelshaus. Solicitor General Robert Bork became acting attorney general and carried out Nixon's order.

Although Nixon broke no law in firing Cox, the incident, which was quickly dubbed the Saturday Night Massacre, made him look all the more guilty. His approval rating dropped to a dismal 17 percent. The public

Deputy Attorney General William Ruckelshaus refused Nixon's order to fire Archibald Cox.

outcry may have influenced his announcement on October 23 that he would turn over the requested tapes. He also announced that a new special prosecutor would be selected. At the suggestion of his chief of staff, Alexander Haig, Nixon appointed Leon Jaworski, a prominent Houston lawyer, to fill the position. Nixon agreed to give Jaworski complete independence in pursuing his investigation.

Nixon launched a campaign to generate positive news to counteract the Watergate stories. On November 17, 1973, he addressed the Associated Press Managing Editors Association in Orlando, Florida. Responding to a question about his tax problems, Nixon said, "I welcome this kind of examination . . . because people have got to know whether or not their President is a crook. Well, I am not a crook. I've earned everything I've got." Political cartoonists and comedians had a field day poking fun at Nixon's remark.

The Tale of the Tapes

As Nixon had feared, the relinquished tapes were creating new and terrible problems for him. On November 21, 1973, it was announced that an 18½-minute gap existed on a tape for June 20, 1972. Someone had erased a conversation that took place in Nixon's office only three days after the Watergate break-in. To most Americans, the silence on the tape was more incriminating than whatever words had been erased.

Nixon continued to fight for control of the remaining tapes. The subpoenas piled up on his desk. He refused to comply with them. In refusing to honor them, Nixon claimed that he was protecting the office for future presidents. He maintained that honoring the subpoenas would destroy the confidentiality of the presidency and weaken the office. There was merit in Nixon's claim, but many Americans believed that he was using the argument to protect himself rather than the office.

When the courts ordered him to comply with subpoenas, his lawyers appealed the decision to the next higher court. One case was eventually appealed all the way to the Supreme Court. For Nixon, the stakes on this appeal were very high. The Supreme Court's decision would be final. If he lost, Nixon would have to give up the tapes. If he still refused, he would be committing a crime.

While the Supreme Court debated his fate, on April 29, Nixon made a bold attempt to satisfy a subpoena issued by the Judiciary Committee of the House of Representatives. He hoped to clear the air on Watergate once and for all and put it behind him. In a televised speech, Nixon announced he was releasing more than twelve hundred pages of edited transcripts of requested tapes. "As far as what the President personally knew and did with regard to Watergate and the cover-up is concerned," Nixon told the television audience, "these materials, together with those already made available, will tell it all."

The effort backfired. The House Judiciary Committee rejected the transcripts and demanded the actual tapes. But Americans devoured the transcripts. For the first time in history, Nixon's silent majority got a glimpse of the brutal game of politics that was played inside the Oval Office and of Nixon's true character. From one transcript, for example, they learned that Nixon betrayed his old friend and campaign

After repeated refusals, Nixon finally released transcripts of White House tapes.

manager John Mitchell in an effort to save himself. Mitchell eventually went to prison. In stark contrast to the public image Nixon cultivated, in private, he was often abusive and explosive. He swore and made ethnic slurs. The transcripts were far more damaging than helpful to Nixon.

Impeachment Hearings

For months, the House Judiciary Committee had been conducting an inquiry on the impeachment of President Nixon. On May 9, the committee began closed hearings on whether Nixon should be impeached. It was only the second time in history the House had undertaken its constitutional responsibility of impeaching a president. President Andrew Johnson, Lincoln's successor, had been impeached in 1868 for firing the secretary of war without the Senate's approval. In doing so, Johnson knowingly violated a law the Congress had just passed. The impeachment process is explicitly outlined in the Constitution. The House of Representatives impeaches or charges the president with specific violations, and then the president is tried in the Senate. A two-thirds majority vote is necessary to secure a conviction on the charges made by the House. Andrew Johnson was not convicted by the Senate.

Hated at Home, Honored Abroad

While the House of Representatives conducted their historic hearings, Nixon struggled to portray himself as a strong president unburdened by Watergate. Although he was suffering from phlebitis, a painful and potentially life-threatening inflammation in his leg, he made a "journey of peace" to the Middle East. When he arrived in Egypt on June 12, more than a million people lined the streets and cheered him. Nixon's reception in Egypt clearly showed he was as popular in other countries as he was hated at home. People abroad could not understand why Americans were making such a fuss over something as trivial as Watergate. To them, whatever illegal activities Nixon may have engaged in paled next to his accomplishments in seeking world peace.

Nixon made additional stops in Syria, Saudi Arabia, Israel, and Jordan, discussing with each country's leader the need for peace in the Middle East. But the news his trip generated had to compete against the latest Watergate news for space on the front pages of U.S. newspapers. He returned to Washington on June 19, one day after his personal attorney, Herb Kalmbach, had been sentenced to six to eighteen months in prison for illegal fund-raising activities on behalf of the White House.

On June 25, Nixon departed for a European trip that included a summit conference in Moscow similar to the one that had produced the SALT agreement two years earlier. Nixon wanted the new summit to cap his detente policy by producing a second disarmament agreement. He was warmly received by Soviet leaders and cheered by Soviet citizens. But it became clear almost immediately that there would be no new arms agreement. Some minor agreements were signed before he returned home, but the summit ended in failure.

The media blamed the failure on Watergate. Nixon himself later blamed other

events. Earlier, the United States had refused to grant special trade status to the Soviet Union, and Americans were sharply critical of the Soviet Union's treatment of its Jewish population. These problems affected the arms negotiations, Nixon argued. He also claimed that the military leaders of both countries actually feared an arms reduction and therefore opposed it.

A Man and a Nation in Crisis

Rumors in Washington surfaced that President Nixon was depressed, even suicidal in the face of the enormous pressure he was under. For months, editorials and politicians had been demanding his resignation. The House of Representatives was hearing evidence for impeachment. *United States v. Nixon,* an appeal of a court order to comply with a subpoena to turn over tapes, was before the Supreme Court. The Senate had just released its scathing report on the Nixon administration. Various criminal trials were revealing more harmful information about Nixon.

Richard Nixon's two-year fight to save himself had thrown the country into crisis. The tremendous boost the national morale had gotten from the end of the Vietnam War had been eroded by two years of Watergate. Under the weight of Watergate proceedings, the government had nearly ground to a halt. The economy, the emerging energy crisis, renewed fighting in Vietnam, continuing tensions in the Middle East, and other pressing domestic and international issues were ignored as the government focused entirely on the growing crisis.

Despite Nixon's efforts, he was unable to negotiate an arms reduction treaty with the Soviet Union in 1974.

Nixon answers questions at a press conference in 1973.

The Smoking Gun

On July 24, 1974, two historic events occurred that signaled the end of Nixon's presidency. The Supreme Court announced its unanimous decision that Nixon had to turn over the subpoenaed tapes to the special prosecutor. The historic ruling recognized the concept of executive privilege but denied Nixon the right to invoke it in criminal cases.

Nixon turned over the requested tapes. Among them was a tape from June 23, 1972, which included Nixon's discussion with Haldeman and their decision to use the CIA to block the FBI investigation of the break-in. The tape became the "smoking gun," the piece of evidence that finally proved that President Nixon had been involved in the cover-up from the very beginning and had been lying to the public for two years.

Also on July 24, the House Judiciary Committee began drafting its articles of impeachment. The first article, passed by the committee on July 27, addressed Watergate.

On June 17, 1972, and prior thereto, agents of the Committee for the Reelection of the President . . . committed unlawful entry of the headquarters of the Democratic National Committee in Washington, District of Columbia, for the purpose of securing political intelligence. Subsequent thereto, Richard M. Nixon, using the powers of his high office, engaged personally and through his subordinates and agents, in a course of conduct or plan designed to delay, impede, and obstruct the investigation of such unlawful entry; to cover up, conceal and protect those responsible; and to conceal the existence and scope of other unlawful covert activities.[26]

Political Confusion

An editorial in the August 10, 1974, issue of the New York Times *criticized Nixon for not being candid about his role in Watergate.*

"Mr. Nixon is no stranger to defeat or adversity, as he has reminded those around him frequently in these last days. It is unfortunate, however, that nowhere in his final public statement did there appear any acknowledgement that something about his own deeds in office might have justified his downfall. He remarked with obvious accuracy that he no longer had a strong enough political base in Congress to complete his term in office. But why had he lost that base?

It would have been far easier for the nation to stress his accomplishments if he himself had shown more candor about his shortcomings.

It need hardly be stressed at this point that the work of analyzing the White House tapes and other evidence of the Watergate conspiracy must go full speed ahead, both for legal determination of guilt or innocence of those already under indictment, and so that future generations can know the validity of the political confusion through which the nation has been dragged."

The article then documented nine "means used to implement this course of conduct." A second article passed on July 29 addressed Nixon's violation of the "constitutional right of citizens" through the misuse of his power as president. A third article citing Nixon's refusal to obey subpoenas issued by the House Judiciary Committee for its investigations was passed on July 30. Each of the three articles ended with the statement: "Wherefore, Richard M. Nixon, by such conduct warrants impeachment and trial, and removal from office."

The End of a Presidency

Nixon knew that his support in the House of Representatives had disappeared and that he would lose the impeachment vote. He also believed that he would be convicted in a Senate trial.

On August 8, Nixon appeared on national television to announce that he would resign. He began by telling the millions of Americans watching that he had always tried to do what was best for the nation. He said it appeared that he did not

Mercy, Not Revenge

Editorial writers found patriotism, sorrow, failure, and deceit in President Nixon's resignation.

"He acted with patriotism, foregoing his own personal desires. For the general good, his decision was the best one he could have made for the country, although it does not resolve many of the questions raised by the Watergate mess." (*Arizona Republic*)

"Our feelings toward Mr. Nixon must be of sorrow rather than anger, and of mercy rather than revenge. His weaknesses are more of blind ambition and poor judgment rather than deliberate contempt for the law." (*Chicago Tribune*)

"Nixon clings to the thought that somehow he could have won 'personal vindication' while only in passing conceding some wrongdoings, apparently unaware of the serious things he did." (*Los Angeles Times*)

"President Nixon had an opportunity to bring the nation together last night and he failed. . . . What everyone waited for was an admission, however slight, of his guilt in the Watergate scandals." (*Miami News*)

"Now Richard Nixon's name will live in obloquy, at least pending some distant work of revisionists which challenges the imagination. . . . In his farewell he was still telling less than the truth to his countrymen." (*Arkansas Gazette*)

Nixon's last morning as president.

Nixon's farewell speech to the cabinet and White House staff.

"have a strong enough political base in the Congress to justify continuing" to serve as president. Echoing his Checkers speech twenty-two years earlier, Nixon declared, "I have never been a quitter." He then said:

> To continue to fight through the months ahead for my personal vindication would almost totally absorb the time and attention of both the President and the Congress in a period when our entire focus should be on the great issues of peace abroad and prosperity without inflation at home.
>
> Therefore, I shall resign the Presidency effective at noon tomorrow. Vice President Ford will be sworn in as President at that hour in this office.[27]

The president expressed his regret for "injuries that may have been done in the course of the events that led to this decision" and claimed that his misjudgments "were made in what I believed at the time to be in the best interest of the Nation." He concluded with a summary of his achievements in his 5½ years as president.

On the morning of August 9, 1974, as the nation watched on television, Nixon and his family walked to a helicopter waiting on the White House lawn. At the top of the steps, Nixon turned to the crowd. He gave an emotional wave and flashed his traditional victory sign and stepped inside. The helicopter rose, carrying the disgraced man and his family to the airport where a jet was waiting to fly them home to California.

At 11:35 A.M., a letter was delivered to Secretary of State Henry Kissinger. "Dear Mr. Secretary," it read, "I hereby resign the Office of President of the United States. Sincerely, Richard Nixon." At noon, Gerald R. Ford was sworn in as the thirty-eighth president of the United States.

Gerald Ford is sworn in as president to complete Nixon's unfinished term.

The Watergate Legacy

The word *Watergate* immediately entered the American language as a synonym for scandal. But Watergate's legacy runs far deeper. In the wake of Watergate, new laws were passed, media coverage of politics changed, the public's distrust of politicians increased, and great shifts in the nation's political landscape took place.

Nixon defended many of his actions by claiming he was trying to protect the office of the presidency. In truth, Nixon's years as president actually weakened the office. His stubborn refusal to cooperate with Congress in both Vietnam and Watergate spurred Congress to enact new laws that limited the powers of future presidents.

The most significant law Congress passed was the War Powers Act. This law limited the president's ability to wage war without congressional approval. President George Bush's actions were governed by this law during the 1991 Persian Gulf War.

Congress also passed other laws in reaction to Nixon and Watergate. The Presidential Records and Materials Preservation

Watergate Deals a Blow

Author Stephen Ambrose described a hidden legacy of Watergate in the concluding book of his three-volume biography of Nixon.

"Because Nixon resigned, the Republican Party moved to the right, bringing a majority of the voters in the country along with it. Watergate discredited Nixon personally while dealing a blow to the 'middle ground' that he had pre-empted in the 1960s between the [liberal] Rockefeller and [conservative] Goldwater forces. When Nixon resigned, the conservatives were free to criticize his policies, which they did. . . . Conservatives [of the Republican party] charged that Nixon had betrayed their cause. . . . When [President] Ford continued Nixon's moderate policies in defense, taxation, and spending, conservatives continued to complain. . . . In 1976, conservatives led a revolt against President Ford, calling for an 'open convention.' They and their allies almost managed to win the 1976 nomination for Reagan. Ford's defeat by Carter gave the conservatives unchallenged control of the Republican Party. This led to major changes in American politics, government, economic affairs, foreign policy, and much more, after Reagan won the 1980 election."

After being accused of an extramarital affair, presidential candidate Gary Hart was forced to halt his campaign.

Act of 1974 placed Nixon's presidential papers in the National Archives, where Nixon is unable to review or amend them. This law contrasts with the Privacy Act of 1974, which permits private citizens to view information about themselves collected in federal agency files and to correct or amend that information.

The Ethics in Government Act of 1978 formally established a permanent, legal basis for the office of special prosecutor in government. Upon appointment, the special prosecutor cannot be removed from his post except by impeachment or conviction of a crime. In an effort to decrease corruption within government, the law also required members of the judicial and executive branches of government to make full financial disclosures about themselves.

Watergate brought other changes to American politics as well. In the post-Nixon years, the investigative reporting methods that helped expose Watergate have played an even larger role in politics. The press more aggressively pursues stories beyond the press conferences and briefings orchestrated by politicians. Politicians themselves are seldom given the benefit of the doubt, and every statement is investigated by the media.

After the fall of Richard Nixon, the media's coverage of presidential campaigns has often focused on the character of the candidates. Politicians' privacy is no longer respected by the media. President Kennedy's alleged infidelities in the early 1960s were not reported out of respect for the man and the office. But in 1988, fourteen years after Watergate, media reports of infidelities of Democratic presidential candidate Gary Hart forced him to drop out of the race.

As a result of Nixon's presidency, the American public has become more cynical about politics. The media's coverage of the private lives of political candidates has nearly destroyed the concept of the politician as hero. Voter turnout has declined in every presidential election since Watergate.

Never in this century have the actions of one man so negatively affected his country. Any other politician would have lived out his life in obscurity and shame. But not Richard Nixon. From the moment he left office in disgrace, Nixon began plotting the ultimate comeback.

8 The Resurrection

Richard Nixon did not quit politics in 1974 because politics was his life. After his resignation from the presidency, Nixon returned to California physically ill and emotionally drained. He faced criminal prosecution for his role in Watergate. He was nearly broke and still had to pay back taxes and astronomical legal bills. Despite his troubles, Nixon would prove his often-spoken claim that he was no quitter. Using the same political skill that had taken him to the top and sent him tumbling to the bottom, Richard Nixon would launch a final comeback, determined to restore his reputation.

His first act as former president was to continue the struggle to secure control of the remaining tapes and other presidential records, which essentially continued the cover-up. Nixon would continue his futile battle for the next seventeen years. In lawsuits filed against the government, Nixon claimed, with some justification, that no president before or since had had such restrictions placed on his presidential papers. But the courts continued to rule against him.

The threat of criminal prosecution evaporated on September 8, 1974, when President Ford announced a full pardon for all illegal activities Nixon may have engaged in during his 5½ years as president. Ford granted the pardon to spare the country further pain about Watergate. But the pardon outraged many Americans, who believed Nixon had been promised the pardon if he would resign. A public opinion poll taken at the time showed that 56 percent of those surveyed favored a criminal trial for the disgraced president.

Nixon issued a brief statement accepting the pardon. He said:

> I was wrong in not acting more decisively and more forthrightly in dealing with

President Ford granted Nixon a full pardon for any illegal activities he may have participated in during his presidency.

Nixon visited China in February 1976, as soon as his health improved and his financial problems were solved.

Watergate, particularly when it reached the stage of judicial proceedings and grew from a political scandal into a national tragedy. No words can describe the depths of my regret and pain at the anguish my mistakes over Watergate have caused the nation and the Presidency—a nation I so deeply love and an institution I so greatly respect.[28]

No pardon could remedy Nixon's medical or financial problems, however. He was hospitalized briefly in September for treatment of his phlebitis. Late in October, doctors discovered an eighteen-inch blood clot in his swollen leg. He underwent immediate surgery. Hours later, he suddenly lapsed into unconsciousness and doctors struggled for several hours to save his life. His recovery was further slowed by pneumonia. Because of his illness, he was unable to return to Washington and testify about his Watergate involvement at the trials of his former aides. The illness spared Nixon from ever having to discuss Watergate while under oath.

To pay his legal and medical bills and his back taxes, Nixon sold two properties in Key Biscayne, Florida, and the publishing rights to his memoirs.

New Goals

As soon as his health permitted, Nixon returned to an active schedule. In February 1976, Nixon accepted an invitation to visit China. The visit was a triumph. Nixon was warmly received by the Chinese and became the first westerner to meet privately with the new Chinese prime minister, Hua Kuo-feng. In a banquet in honor of Nixon, the prime minister acknowledged Nixon's importance to U.S.-China relations.

Four years ago, President Nixon visited our country, and China and the United States issued the famous Shanghai communique. That historic event has played a major role in improving and developing Sino-U.S. relations and exerted a far-reaching influence internationally. Mr. Nixon certainly showed farsightedness in taking this courageous action in his capacity as U.S. President at a time when contacts between the Chinese and American peoples had been suspended for more than 20 years.[29]

After his return to the United States, Nixon was called secretly by Secretary of State Henry Kissinger, who sought Nixon's observations about his trip. The call showed that Nixon's political observations were still valued. Its secrecy, however, indicated that the Ford administration needed to avoid public association with Nixon because of the Watergate disgrace. Nixon understood. Throughout the 1976 campaign, Nixon worked behind the scenes for Ford's reelection. He fed President Ford a steady stream of information, ranging from the names of old political contacts to tips on how to improve his appearance.

Nixon had another, more negative impact on the 1976 election. Ford lost the election to Jimmy Carter by a narrow margin. Exit polls showed that about 7 percent of the voters had chosen Carter because Ford had pardoned Nixon.

Out of Exile

In 1977, Nixon ventured once again into the public spotlight. Needing money to pay off his remaining expenses, he appeared on four televised interviews with David Frost, which earned him $540,000. The highlight of the interviews came when Frost asked Nixon if he would go beyond admitting "mistakes" about Watergate. Frost said that Americans wanted Nixon to admit to wrongdoing, and abusing his power and to apologize for the two years of agony he caused. But Nixon remained defiant. "People didn't think it was enough to admit mistakes. Fine. If they want me to get down and grovel on the floor, no. Never. Because I don't believe I should."

The year 1978 was a turning point in Nixon's comeback. In January, he returned to Washington for the first time since his resignation to attend a memorial service for Hubert H. Humphrey, his opponent in the 1968 presidential election. He remained in Washington for only a few hours. He did not speak to the press.

That year, Nixon published *RN: The Memoirs of Richard Nixon*. The book covered his entire life but emphasized his years as president. The book became a best-seller, launching Nixon on a new career as an author. Nixon proved to be as controversial in print as he had always been in person. His defense of his Vietnam policy, especially his reasons for the Christmas bombings, was called self-serving

Nixon attends the memorial service for Hubert Humphrey.

Nixon declares his return to politics in Biloxi, Mississippi in November 1978.

by some reviewers. Nixon discussed Watergate in detail. Some reviewers found a confession of his involvement in the cover-up, while others claimed he continued to deny his guilt.

Late in 1978, Nixon began accepting speaking engagements. Addressing the American Legion in Biloxi, Mississippi, on November 11, Nixon declared he was "out" of exile.

Growing Influence

Nixon continued his comeback by traveling widely. He was enthusiastically received by foreign leaders, who remained puzzled by Nixon's unpopularity in his own country. To these leaders, Nixon was a great statesman. He began to speak out on foreign affairs in opinion pieces published in newspapers and magazines.

He became a prolific author, turning out books and articles on foreign policy issues. His favorite topic continued to be communism and the Soviet Union. In *The Real War,* published in 1980, Nixon argued that detente was no longer a valid policy. He now favored a more hard-line approach against the buildup of Soviet arms. How much this book influenced President Ronald Reagan is hard to determine. It is a fact, however, that three years after Nixon's book appeared, Reagan instituted his own hard-line approach to the Soviet Union, which he called an "evil empire."

Leaders, published in 1982, profiled a series of great world leaders Nixon had met during his long career, including Winston Churchill, Charles de Gaulle, Nikita Khrushchev, and Chinese leader Chou Enlai. Nixon described the contributions of each leader to his times and then added his own reflections and memories about each individual. This book is often called Nixon's best.

Nixon's influence as an adviser continued to grow. Politicians, including President Reagan, privately sought out his advice. Reagan and Nixon remained in contact throughout Reagan's two terms in office. It is difficult to determine how much Nixon actually influenced Reagan's policies. Nixon, in turn, sought out the politicians. Regularly, he forwarded memos and articles containing his observations on current events to key members of government.

In 1983, Nixon self-published *Real Peace: A Strategy for the West* and sent copies at his own expense to government leaders and officials. Readers found that Nixon's

Nixon was not publicly accepted by the Republican party, even though he privately advised President Ronald Reagan.

approach to the Soviet Union had evolved further. He combined his earlier positions and advocated "hard-headed detente," a combination of detente and deterrence. Again, Nixon's influence on foreign policy is hard to measure. However, just as *The Real War* preceded Reagan's hard-line stance against the Soviet Union, *Real Peace* preceded the softening of Reagan's Soviet policy.

By 1984, the tenth anniversary of his resignation, Nixon had come a long way from the day he had left Washington in disgrace. Despite his steadily growing influence, his return was not complete. Nixon had won back the private respect of most Republicans and some Democrats as well. Publicly, however, the Republican party still excluded him from the 1984 Republican national convention, just as it had in 1976 and 1980. Many Americans still refused to forgive him for Watergate, primarily because Nixon still refused to admit his guilt.

Nixon continued to work toward the restoration of his reputation in his own way. In 1985, he published *No More Vietnams,* a subjective history of the Vietnam War. The book had both strengths and weaknesses. In it, Nixon argued that the real message of Vietnam was not to avoid fighting wars in the future but to make the right decisions and avoid *losing* them. This argument reflected the country's changing attitudes about the Vietnam experience, once again demonstrating Nixon's ability to reflect the public mood.

The book was weakened by Nixon's defense of his own Vietnam policies, while shifting blame for failure to others. He blamed the final fall of South Vietnam two years after the United States signed the 1973 treaty on the refusal of Congress to grant aid to South Vietnam to continue its fight. He avoided putting responsibility on China and the Soviet Union, which had continued to arm North Vietnam.

"He's Back"

Despite the criticisms his book received, Nixon's popularity continued to increase. In April 1986 he earned a standing ovation after his speech to the American Newspaper Publishers Association about world affairs. The cameras clicked as Nixon shook hands with Katharine Graham, publisher of the *Washington Post,* the newspaper whose investigative stories had helped expose Watergate and force Nixon's resignation.

Fierce Determination

John Herbers commented on Richard Nixon's recovery in the August 5, 1984, issue of the New York Times *on the tenth anniversary of Nixon's resignation from the presidency.*

"A decade [after his resignation, Nixon] has emerged at 71 years of age as an elder statesman, commentator on foreign and domestic affairs, advisor to world leaders, a multimillionaire and a successful author and lecturer honored by audiences at home and abroad.

Yet despite his remarkable recovery, much of it a result of his fierce determination to survive as a respected public figure, friends and foes alike agree that his rehabilitation has not been complete. . . .

Mr. Nixon's inability to totally shed the stigma of Watergate after 10 years is one indication of the lasting impact of the scandals that infested his Administration. According to a range of academic and political authorities, Watergate in its broadest sense made a major mark on American politics and government.

He tells friends he has changed and mellowed. But some who have known him over the years say he is still the same person with essentially the same traits and opinions he displayed in public life. In numerous public appearances he has steadfastly refused to admit guilt in the Watergate crimes, attributing his failure to faulty judgements. In private, he still talks about his enemies: liberals, academics, the press, Easterners in the Ivy League."

Nixon regained political influence, but never lost the stain of Watergate.

"What Makes the Guy Tick?"

The May 19, 1986, issue of Newsweek *featured Richard Nixon's comments on his comeback and what he represented to people twelve years after his resignation.*

"They're here because they want to hear what I have to say, but they're [also] here because they say, 'What makes this guy tick?' They see me and they think, 'He's come back' or 'He's risen from the dead.'. . . There's only one No. 1. There are more that are not No. 1 than are No. 1. There are more that have suffered defeat than have not, so what I in a sense represent is that defeat does not kill unless the individual gives up. It was vitally important to have something to live for. I would say that what was very helpful to me in the first years was I had a huge project in those memoirs. . . . I get letters all the time that say, 'We just want you to know we're still for you despite what happened, you weren't any worse than any of the others.'"

In May 1986, a cover story in *Newsweek* magazine announced that Nixon was rehabilitated.

He's back. It's hard to say what finally signifies redemption for a disgraced president, the first ever to resign the office: Is it writing an article on summitry for *Foreign Affairs,* and having Ronald Reagan telephone for advice? Is it appearing on Rolling Stone's list of "Who's Hot: The New Stars in Your Future"? Is it getting a standing ovation from the American Newspaper Publishers Association, or being asked to arbitrate a labor dispute that threatened to disrupt the World Series, or being besieged by autograph seekers on a casual Burger King pit stop in New Jersey? Richard Milhous Nixon has done all those things and more in recent months; at 73, he is well launched in yet another new life.[30]

Elder Statesman

Through hard work and careful timing, Richard Nixon had become the nation's elder statesman. He was again a public figure, an author, a lecturer, and an adviser to the nation's leaders. He spoke out on the current issues of the day.

In 1989, Nixon played a key role in communicating the Bush administration's disapproval of the Chinese government's brutal suppression of pro-democracy demonstrations in Tiananmen Square. Nixon consulted with President Bush, then flew as a private citizen to China in late October. Because of his personal relationship with the Chinese, Nixon was able to be blunt. He told the Chinese leaders that the massacre of students at Tiananmen Square had thrown the relationship between the two countries into a critical stage, the most critical since communications were reestablished in 1972. China, Nixon warned his hosts, must not become a "backwater of suppression." Upon his return to the United States, he briefed Bush on his visit. A *New York Times* editorial for November 4, 1989, praised "tough minded" Richard Nixon for telling China "the hard truth." Two days later, noted political columnist William Safire wrote in the same newspaper that "only Nixon . . . had the credentials . . . to express our outrage at the Tiananmen massacre."

As the decade changed, Nixon continued to churn out books. After the sudden collapse of the Soviet Union in 1991, Nixon produced a new book, *Seize the Moment: America's Challenge in a One-Superpower World,* published early in 1992. Nixon argued that despite the collapse of its old enemy, the United States should continue to provide peace and stability in the world by maintaining its own strength. In March 1992, Nixon advocated assistance to the former Soviet Union in an article for *Time* magazine entitled "We Are Ignoring Our World Role."

> In the cold war, we helped avoid great evils. But now we have the chance to advance great goods. While the communists have lost, we have not won until we prove that the ideas of freedom can provide the peoples of the former Soviet Union with a better life. We must enlist the same spirit that won the defensive battle against communism to win the offensive battle to ensure the victory of freedom. We must mobilize the West to commit the billions of dollars needed to give Russia's reforms a fighting chance to succeed.[31]

That same month, Nixon made a speech that criticized President Bush and the Democratic presidential candidates for ignoring foreign policy issues during the 1992 campaign. The speech, of course, also served to promote his new book. Nixon's influence on

Nixon meets with Chinese leader Deng Xiaoping (far left) in 1989.

Nixon greets workers during his 1989 visit to China.

George Bush followed Nixon's advice when he proposed an aid program for the new Commonwealth of Independent States.

the candidates was unmistakable. They obviously respected his views and knew that many Americans did as well. Within days, both Bush and the leading Democratic presidential candidate, Bill Clinton, proposed aid programs for the Commonwealth of Independent States.

Epilogue

Richard Nixon's determined efforts to rehabilitate himself and assume a new role as an influential elder statesman were successful. Twenty years after the Watergate burglary, Nixon is more popular than ever before. In the United States and around the world, he is acknowledged and respected as an expert in international issues. His views appear regularly in newspapers and magazines. Even though he holds no official position, Nixon is able to influence politicians in both parties, as he did when he criticized presidential candidates for ignoring the fallen Soviet Union.

Despite his successful rehabilitation, Nixon has not been able to shed his disgraceful association with Watergate. A survey of forty-nine leading historians published in the *Chicago Tribune* in 1982 rated American presidents in the categories of leadership, accomplishments, political skill, appointments, and character. Eight years after Watergate, the historians rated Nixon fourth from last among the presidents evaluated. When these same historians were asked to list the ten worst presidents, they listed Nixon next to last. While some acknowledged his foreign policy accomplishments, most felt that Watergate outweighed his achievements and that Nixon would forever be remembered as the only president forced to resign from office.

Governor Bill Clinton demonstrated his respect for Nixon's political views during the 1992 presidential campaign by following some of his recommendations about relations with the Commonwealth of Independent States.

A Continued Fascination

A syndicated column by Joseph R. L. Sterne appearing in the March 25, 1992, issue of the Min- neapolis, Minnesota- based Star-Tribune *commented on Nixon's current and future place in history.*

"Of our four living ex-presidents, Richard Nixon is first in point of service and last in the hearts of his country- men. . . . He not only fancies himself an expert on for- eign policy; he is an expert on the subject, a man more highly respected outside than inside his own country. . . . Future historians, I suspect, will give Nixon high marks not only for his foreign policy but for his liberal—repeat liberal—social agenda implementing the Johnson Great Society. His funding for social programs infuriates Rea- ganites to this day. . . . Nixon is enormously complicated and engrossing. He is domineering yet tortured by self- doubt, crude yet intellectually fastidious. He will fasci- nate Americans long after most other 20th century presi- dents have become names on a list."

As recently as 1991, historians were still judging Nixon harshly. Historian Stephen E. Ambrose, author of a three-volume biog- raphy of the former president, wrote in 1991 that Nixon could have been a great president, but "he doesn't even rate as a good one. He is the only President who re- signed from office, the only one forced to accept a pardon for his deeds. This will never be forgotten."

The former president himself recog- nizes the disastrous effect Watergate had on his presidency. "Without the Watergate episode," he told *Newsweek* in 1986, "I would be rated, I should think, rather high. Without it. With it, it depends upon who's doing the rating."

Regardless of how future historians rate Nixon, they will most certainly recognize his importance. Richard Nixon has been ar- guably the most important American politi- cian of the second half of the twentieth cen- tury. In nearly fifty years as a public figure, Nixon has been both a positive and a nega- tive force in American and world politics. But his achievements have always been offset by his questionable moral character. In the end, Nixon created one of the largest politi- cal scandals in American history and left the nation with a bitter legacy. As the Watergate scandal fades with time, however, future his- torians will no doubt reinterpret the impor- tance of Nixon's accomplishments as they continue to influence world politics.

Notes

Chapter 1: Young Richard Nixon

1. Hannah Nixon, "Richard Nixon: A Mother's Story," *Good Housekeeping,* June 1960.
2. Richard Nixon, *RN: The Memoirs of Richard Nixon.* Vol. 1. New York: Warner Books, 1978.
3. Hannah Nixon, *Good Housekeeping.*
4. Roger Morris, *Richard Milhous Nixon: The Rise of an American Politician.* New York: Henry Holt, 1990.
5. Hannah Nixon, *Good Housekeeping.*
6. Morris, *Richard Milhous Nixon.*

Chapter 2: The Rise to Power

7. Richard Nixon, *RN: The Memoirs of Richard Nixon.* Vol. 1.
8. Jerry Voorhis, *The Strange Case of Richard Milhous Nixon.* New York: Popular Library, 1973.
9. Richard Nixon, *RN: The Memoirs of Richard Nixon.* Vol. 1.
10. Richard Nixon, *RN: The Memoirs of Richard Nixon.* Vol. 1.

Chapter 3: Toward the Vice-Presidency

11. Reprinted in *New York Times,* September 21, 1952.
12. Richard Nixon, "My Side of the Story," *Vital Speeches of the Day,* October 15, 1952.

Chapter 4: Richard Nixon, Vice-President

13. Richard Nixon, *RN: The Memoirs of Richard Nixon.* Vol. 1.
14. Richard Nixon, *RN: The Memoirs of Richard Nixon.* Vol. 1.
15. Richard Nixon, *RN: The Memoirs of Richard Nixon.* Vol. 1.
16. Richard Nixon, *RN: The Memoirs of Richard Nixon.* Vol. 1.

Chapter 5: Running for President

17. Richard Nixon, *RN: The Memoirs of Richard Nixon.* Vol. 1.
18. Richard Nixon, *RN: The Memoirs of Richard Nixon.* Vol. 1.
19. Richard Nixon, *RN: The Memoirs of Richard Nixon.* Vol. 1.
20. Richard Nixon, *RN: The Memoirs of Richard Nixon.* Vol. 1.

Chapter 6: Foreign Policy

21. Richard Nixon, "Cambodia: A Difficult Decision," *Vital Speeches of the Day,* May 15, 1970.
22. Richard Nixon, *RN: The Memoirs of Richard Nixon.* Vol. 1.
23. *New York Times,* January 24, 1973.

Chapter 7: Watergate: The Fall

24. *New York Times* staff, *The End of a Presidency.* New York: Bantam Books, 1973.
25. *New York Times* staff, *The White House Transcripts.* New York: Bantam Books, 1974.
26. *New York Times* staff, *The End of a Presidency.*
27. Richard Nixon, *Public Papers of the Presidents of the United States, Containing the Public Messages, Speeches, and Statements of the President, January 1-August 9, 1974.* Washington, DC: Government Printing Office, 1975.

Chapter 8: The Resurrection

28. *New York Times,* September 9, 1974.
29. *Peking Review,* February 27, 1976.
30. *Newsweek,* May 19, 1986.
31. *Time,* March 16, 1992.

For Further Reading

Roger Barr, *The Vietnam War.* San Diego: Lucent Books, 1991.

Fred J. Cook, *The Crimes of Watergate.* New York: Watts, 1981.

Jim Hargrove, *Richard M. Nixon: The Thirty-seventh President.* Chicago: Children's Press, 1985.

Harry Nickelson, *Vietnam.* San Diego: Lucent Books, 1989.

Hannah Nixon, as told to Fiora Rheta Schreiber, "Richard Nixon: A Mother's Story," *Good Housekeeping,* June 1960.

Sallie Randolph, *Richard M. Nixon, President.* New York: Walker, 1989.

Peter C. Ripley, *Richard Nixon.* New York: Chelsea House, 1987.

Bob Woodward and Carl Bernstein, *All the President's Men.* New York: Warner Paperback Library, 1975.

Bob Woodward and Carl Bernstein, *The Final Days.* New York: Avon Books, 1976.

Works Consulted

The following is a partial listing of major sources consulted by the author in the preparation of this book.

Books

Stephen E. Ambrose, *Nixon: Ruin and Recovery, 1973-1990.* New York: Simon & Schuster, 1991. This concluding volume of a three-volume biography of Nixon covers the end of the Vietnam War, Watergate, and Nixon's postpresidential years.

Fawn M. Brodie, *Richard Nixon: The Shaping of His Character.* New York: W.W. Norton, 1981. An exploration of the development of Nixon's character, this volume traces many of Nixon's behavioral patterns from childhood into his politi-cal career. The volume ends with Kennedy's assassination. This is a controversial, mostly negative work about Nixon.

Whittaker Chambers, *Witness.* Washington, DC: Regnery Gateway, 1952. The former communist whose testimony exposed Alger Hiss offers his side of the story.

Congressional Quarterly's Guide to the U.S. Supreme Court. 2nd ed. Washington, DC: Government Printing Office, 1990. This reference work covers the history of the Supreme Court, including Nixon's four appointments.

Helen Gahagan Douglas, *A Full Life.* Garden City, NY: Doubleday, 1982. Douglas's autobiography includes her account of the 1950 Senate race in which she was defeated by Richard Nixon.

The Gallup Poll, Public Opinion 1972-1977. Wilmington, DE: Scholarly Resources, 1978. Public opinion polls conducted by Gallup, including many on Nixon's popularity, are summarized in this reference work.

Alger Hiss, *In the Court of Public Opinion.* New York: Knopf, 1957. Convicted perjurer Alger Hiss tells his side of the infamous spy case that brought Richard Nixon national recognition.

Roger Morris, *Richard Milhous Nixon: The Rise of an American Politician.* New York: Henry Holt, 1990. A superbly detailed account of Nixon's life from birth up to his 1953 inauguration as vice-president of the United States. Rich in detail and historical perspective, this volume takes great pains to treat Nixon fairly, yet Nixon's negative side is well documented. It is perhaps the best account of his early career yet written.

Robert K. Murry and Tim H. Blessing, *Greatness in the White House: Rating the Presidents, Washington through Carter.* University Park: Pennsylvania State University Press, 1988. An expanded version of the authors' 1983 article in the *Journal of American History.*

New York Times staff, *The End of a Presidency,* New York: Bantam Books, 1973. A day-by-day chronicle of the last months of Nixon's presidency and the events that forced his resignation. Commentary by the *Times* staff and transcripts of important tapes are also included.

New York Times staff, *The White House Transcripts.* New York: Bantam Books, 1974. The text of important presidential tapes as reprinted by the *Times.* Includes the infamous "cancer on the presidency" tape of March 21, 1973.

Richard Nixon, *Public Papers of the Presidents of the United States, Containing the Public Messages, Speeches, and Statements of the President, January 1–9, 1974.* Washington, DC: Government Printing Office, 1975. The complete text of President Nixon's August 8, 1974, resignation speech and his remarks before departing the White House on August 9.

Richard Nixon, *RN: The Memoirs of Richard Nixon.* New York: Grosset and Dunlap, 1978. Richard Nixon tells his life's story with heavy emphasis on his years as president. His accounts of controversial subjects often minimalize his role, defend his position, or simply exclude unflattering events altogether. Nevertheless, Nixon is often candid in sharing his feelings about the most important events in his career. These memoirs should be supplemented with careful outside research.

Richard Nixon, *Six Crises.* Garden City, NY: Doubleday, 1962. Nixon discusses the major events of his early career (the Hiss case, the Fund Crisis, Eisenhower's heart attack, his trip to South America, debating Khrushchev, and the 1960 presidential election) in more detail than he does in his later memoirs.

Herbert S. Parmet. *Richard Nixon and His America.* Boston: Little, Brown, 1990. This one-volume biography of Nixon is the most favorable of those written since Nixon resigned.

This Fabulous Century, 1950–1960. Alexandria, VA: Time Life Books, 1970. An overview of the 1950s, including coverage of the rise and fall of McCarthyism.

Jerry Voorhis, *The Strange Case of Richard Milhous Nixon.* New York: Popular Library, 1973. Voorhis was Nixon's first political opponent in 1946 and was easily defeated. In this scathing look at Nixon, Voorhis gets his revenge.

Periodicals

John Herbers, "After Decade, Nixon Is Gaining Favor," *New York Times,* August 5, 1984. This brief *New York Times* article reviews Nixon's standing in society and politics ten years after his resignation.

Robert K. Murry and Tim H. Blessing, "The Presidential Performance Study: A Progress Report," *Journal of American History,* December 1983. A scholarly review of the authors' methods for rating presidential performance and a ranking of all U.S. presidents through Jimmy Carter.

Steve Neal, "Our Best and Worst Presidents," *Chicago Tribune Sunday Magazine,*

January 10, 1982. Discusses Nixon's performance as president and his ranking in relationship to other American presidents.

Newsweek, May 19, 1986. Cover story is devoted to Nixon's rehabilitation after his resignation and offers Nixon's own assessment of why people remain interested in him.

New York Times, September 21, 1952. News coverage and editorials surrounding the 1952 Fund Crisis that nearly ended Nixon's campaign for the vice-presidency.

Richard Nixon, "My Side of the Story," *Vital Speeches of the Day,* October 15, 1952. National television speech delivered September 23, 1952, defending his special fund for Senate expenses.

Richard Nixon, "We Are Ignoring Our World Role," *Time,* April 13, 1992. A brief article in which Nixon outlines his views on the U.S. role in the world after the collapse of the Soviet Union.

Joseph R. L. Sterne, "Nearing 80, Nixon Remains Complex, Engrossing Man," *Minneapolis Star-Tribune,* March 25, 1992. This brief column compliments Nixon on his foreign policy expertise and argues that Nixon will be remembered more positively by future historians.

Index

Picture Credits

About the Author

Roger Barr is a free-lance writer, book reviewer, and editor who lives in Saint Paul, Minnesota. He has written widely on historical and cultural subjects for various regional magazines. His book reviews appear frequently in the *Saint Paul Pioneer Press*. He is the author of *The Vietnam War* for Lucent Books and of a forthcoming novel entitled *The Treasure Hunt*.